Stories, Quips, and Quotes
to Lift the Heart

hum♥R
for a
w♥man's heart

Compiled by Shari MacDonald
Illustrated by Kristen Myers

HOWARD
PUBLISHING CO.

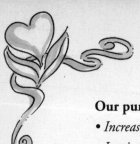

Our purpose at Howard Publishing is to:

• *Increase faith* in the hearts of growing Christians

• *Inspire holiness* in the lives of believers

• *Instill hope* in the hearts of struggling people everywhere

Because He's coming again!

Published by Howard Publishing Co., Inc.,
3117 North 7th Street, West Monroe, Louisiana 71291-2227

ISBN 0-7394-2338-X

Compiled by Shari MacDonald
Cover art by Vanessa Bearden
Illustrated by Kristen Myers
Interior design by Stephanie Denney

Contents

chapter 4: ten laughs, no weighting

chapter 5: parenting—not for the faint of heart or the slow to laugh

chapter 6: blushing beauties —embarrassing moments

chapter 7: laughter, family style

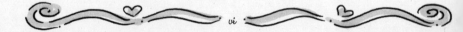

chapter 12: how quickly they grow, how swiftly we laugh

chapter 13: you've got to be kidding —more family humor

chapter 14: mother, may i laugh?

chapter 15: ignorance is (domestic) bliss

just **kidding** around

What about the Grownups?

—FROM THE BEST OF THE GOOD CLEAN JOKES
BY BOB PHILLIPS

"Daddy, I want to ask you a question," said little Bobby after his first day in Sunday school.

"Yes, Bobby, what is it?"

"The teacher was reading the Bible to us—all about the children of Israel building the temple, the children of Israel crossing the Red Sea, the children of Israel making sacrifices. Didn't the grownups do anything?"

The Cheez Doodle Principle
Nancy Kennedy

Recently, I estimated that I've packed 2,179 school lunches.

That's something like 1,084 peanut butter and jelly sandwiches, 829 tuna, 45 egg salad, 143 bologna and 78 unidentified. Only 1,822 of those were actually eaten by my children.

Of the 2,179 carefully packed pieces of fruit I've lovingly included for balanced nutrition, I'd say most, if not all, are now compost at the bottom of some landfill. Add the thousands of carrot sticks, dozens of cherry tomatoes and scores of cheese chunks that go directly from lunch box to trash can, and I have 2,179 reasons to sleep in.

The only foods I'm certain get eaten are the factory-packaged, artificially colored and flavored, chemical infested, sugar- and fat-laden goodies that I warn the lunch-box carrier not to eat until after the healthy stuff is gone (which kids define as wadded

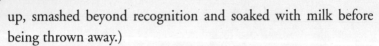

up, smashed beyond recognition and soaked with milk before being thrown away.)

That leaves me to conclude that if you are what you eat, then my children are Cheez Doodles and Ho-Ho's.

I have other options in the Lunch Box Game. I could stay in bed, forget about packing lunches, and look like the Joan Crawford of all mothers—or pack what they do eat—namely, junk food. That might win points with my kids, but word would leak out and I'd become the dreaded "other kids' mom," as in, "Other kids' moms pack candy bars and fried pies in *their* lunch boxes."

I could make them eat cafeteria food, but as I've been duly told, "Cafeteria food is garooosss." Case closed.

That leaves packing the lunch box.

As a veteran packer, I've observed several Lunch-Box Laws and Principles:

> If you are what you eat, then my children are Cheez Doodles and Ho-Ho's.

The Law of Negative Consumption. Simply stated, expensive sandwich fillings such as roast beef or honey-glazed ham never get eaten. Out-of-season fruit gets sat upon on the bus. The last bagel that you secretly coveted but gave to your child gets immediately drenched in red Hawaiian Punch.

The Law of Unbearable Temptation. This occurs whenever a child is confronted with a food having a higher playwithability factor than eatability factor. These include raisins, which get arranged barricade-style then flicked across the table; bananas, which are used as guns and/or nonreturnable boomerangs; and

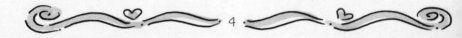

marshmallows, which occasionally get eaten, but only after the child stuffs them all into his cheeks at once.

The Law of Leakability. This law states that even if you wrap your child's field-trip permission slip/report card/school picture carefully in triple plastic bags before putting it inside his lunch box, his leak-proof factory-sealed boxed drink will leak, destroying everything in its wake.

The Law of "Oh, No!" Under this law, soda in a thermos explodes, Jell-O melts and mustard permanently attaches itself to white clothing.

The Principle of "Go Figure." Ziploc bags neither zip nor lock when in a child's possession. Metal spoons and expensive plastic containers never come home, but disposable plastic spoons and Cool Whip containers do. The same kid who won't eat a broken potato chip at home will smash a bag of chips into chip dust—then eat it with a spoon. Go Figure.

There is a bright side. Even if my children never eat the thousands of lunches I pack for them during their school careers, my efforts are not in vain. Colossians 3:23–24 reminds me: "Whatever you do, work at it with all your heart, as working for the Lord, not for men, since you know that you will receive an inheritance from the Lord as a reward."

There's also an end in sight—my last child graduates next year. Until then, I'll just take things one day at a time. Meanwhile, pass the Cheez Doodles—the bus is almost here.

The Big Boo
from the Balcony

Gwendolyn Mitchell Diaz

This story took place several years ago—long enough that I can relate it to you without total embarrassment (and maybe even with a giggle). It took place one Sunday morning at church. Actually, it started the day before at the ball field....

You see, some friends of ours had given us tickets to a Detroit Tigers spring training game. It was the first adult baseball game that our four boys had ever been to, and they took it in with wide eyes and open ears. They were fascinated by everything—the batting practice, the foul balls that flew over their heads, the hot dogs in the "squished" buns, the cheering, the booing...yes, particularly the booing.

Not only was it their first real baseball game, it was the first time in their lives that our boys had ever been exposed to real-life booing. And the man in the seat behind Matthew was indeed a

master boo-er. He booed EVERYTHING from the groundskeepers to the managers; from the umpires to the hot dog vendors. And he did it all with great gusto.

Matthew, who was about five years old at the time, was entranced. For the first few innings, he just sat there staring back at the big booing mouth behind him. About halfway through the fifth inning, however, he decided to get in on the action, and cued by the gentleman (I use the term loosely) behind him, he became a bona fide boo-er. It was all rather funny and cute…until the next day.

Our church is very large and very proper. We happened to be celebrating our 100th anniversary. It was a very special service with bell choirs, bagpipes, and red-robed ensembles, so I decided it would be a good idea to take the children into the sanctuary with me instead of depositing them in children's church as usual. My husband was out of town (of course), so the children and I sneaked quietly into a corner of the balcony.

> We all stood
> and clapped.
> All except for
> one of us,
> that is.

After many beautiful, but rather lengthy, musical selections, an elder of the church began to introduce everyone who had been a member of the church for fifty years or more. You wouldn't believe how many people fit into that category. The list went on and on.

We had been asked to hold our applause until the end, so when the long list was finally completed, we all stood and clapped very formally, very decently, very properly. All except for one of us, that is. Louder than all the thousands of clapping hands was—you guessed it—the sound of Matthew booing

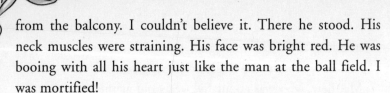

from the balcony. I couldn't believe it. There he stood. His neck muscles were straining. His face was bright red. He was booing with all his heart just like the man at the ball field. I was mortified!

As I said, this happened several years ago. Matthew is now nineteen and has learned to boo a little more appropriately. He is even allowed back in church on rare occasions.

Last week, I actually laughed as a friend and I recalled the event. I didn't turn red or stumble for excuses or blame the man at the stadium. I just plain laughed out loud. It was nice to realize that time not only matures our children in stature and wisdom—time also has a sense of humor. And, given enough time, even mortification can have its moment of mirth.

George Invades Cyberspace

Charlene Ann Baumbich

My husband signed up to take a beginning computer class. I, his wife of 26 years, was stunned yet proud. You see, George likes things the way they are, and technology doesn't.

George likes to watch TV in his recliner. He sometimes likes to add longhand. He likes to drink generic green pop he buys at a warehouse place. He likes his old sport jacket that has an unremovable spot—certified by dry cleaners everywhere—because it goes with his black polyester pants that stretch just where he needs them to. I'm telling you, "creativity" is not his middle name.

Meanwhile, I, his high-tech wife, am on my third computer. I love cutting-edge gadgets and high-speed electronics. I love to buy one-of-a kind outrageous outfits—sans polyester—that make me feel fashionably trendy.

I had tried for years to talk George into taking a computer class, since we both knew it wouldn't be a good idea for me to teach him. Patience is nowhere to be seen among my virtues, and we value our relationship. Besides, I thought if he took a class, he could teach *me* some behind-the-screen details.

But when George finally signed up, a part of me panicked. "Uh-oh!" I thought. "He's going to want to practice on *my* computer!" My book manuscripts and magazine articles and business correspondence lurk in the bowels of my machine. My proposals and committee reports and public relations stuff are all on standby awaiting speedy printout.

I imagined George dinking around with my computer, and fear gripped me. What if he wiped out the last two years of my life? Then I took comfort, figuring my low-tech husband would change his mind about the course. But he didn't.

> I felt like I was abandoning my innocent baby in the arms of Godzilla.

George hurried home from work to take a shower before his big date with Mr. Megabyte. The computer class was in a town ten minutes away. But George left an hour and fifteen minutes early, just to make sure. It had been a long while since I'd witnessed my husband's vulnerability. It was kind of endearing.

Later that night, we talked about the class. "I'll have to practice when I get home tomorrow," he said. "Show me how to use your computer tonight so I'll be ready."

Uh-oh. "George," I stalled, "I've been at my computer all day. The last thing I want to do is boot up at bedtime." Thinking fast,

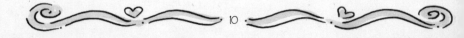

I added, "You're probably on information overload anyway." George agreed, and the invasion was diverted.

Mid-morning the next day, he called me from work. "You gonna be home tonight? I need you to show me how to use your computer before I forget what I learned. I especially need to practice the keyboard." George had never learned to type.

"No, I have a meeting," I explained. "I don't think it would be a good idea for you to be here alone without instructions." Promises were made for the *next* day.

He called again the same time the following day. There was no getting out of this one, even though I did have to go out that evening. Before I left the house, I opened a file for him and explained what *not* to do. A few quick trials were run. Tension mounted.

"Just don't touch 'file'!" I pleaded. I felt like I was abandoning my innocent baby in the arms of Godzilla. During my entire meeting that night, I imagined the worst about what I might discover when I got home. I checked my watch every few minutes, envisioning George innocently bringing on a systems failure. Hard drive crashed. All files lost.

I expected to see "You're in B-I-G trouble, Bucko!" blinking on the computer screen.

When I rushed in the front door the house was quiet. George was already in bed. I ran up the stairs to my office, straining to hear the familiar hum of my computer. My heart pounded as I sat down, took a deep breath, ever so gently put my hand on the mouse and moved it to the right. The screen-saver pattern blinked off—and what I discovered was the last thing I expected: an aspect of George that even after 26 years I never knew existed.

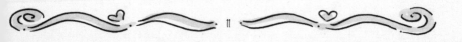

My practical, nuts-and-bolts husband had been practicing his word processing. He wrote, "As I'm typing, you'd think the words were flying onto the screen at record pace and blurring speed. Wrong. I'm typing the way a chicken pecks at grains of food, one by one—only not as fast. On the screen, it looks like a professional did it. *Only we know who really did!*"

It was cute. It was funny. It was kind of charming. It was even poetic. My George, known to some of our friends as Garage Man, was writing with metaphors and communicating with humor and personality in typed words. It was a creative side of my husband I'd never seen.

A couple of weeks later he brought home a printout of a graphic. It was a detailed flowering plant with a bee buzzing around it.

"Cool," I said. "Did you find this in a clip-art file and import it?"

"No. I just drew what was in my head."

On the cutting edge of technology—a place I never thought I'd find my husband—I saw a gift I never knew he had. It was one more thing to love about my "steady" man—the steady, creative man whose hidden talent surfaced on *my* computer.

I'm sure glad he didn't change his mind about taking that class.

three laughs for mom

Go Figure
—DAVE BARRY

If a woman has to choose between catching a fly ball and saving an infant's life, she will choose to save the infant's life without even considering if there are men on base.

Everyone Else's Mom

Gwendolyn Mitchell Diaz

There is someone I'm dying to meet. You've probably heard about her. She's the hero of our younger generation. They mention her just about every day using nothing but praise and adulation. It is always with intense feeling and great admiration that they speak of her.

No, I'm not referring to the latest movie star or the hottest new super model. I'm talking about that someone they refer to as "Everyone Else's Mom." From what I can tell, she must be quite a gal.

You see, Everyone Else's Mom lets her kids stay up past 11:00 P.M. on weeknights and as late as they want on weekends. She agrees with them that sleep is just a waste of life. (I guess her kids never get grouchy.)

Everyone Else's Mom doesn't care if her kids comb their hair or wear belts to hold up their pants when they leave for school. She allows plenty of room in their lives for freedom of expression. Everyone Else's Mom lets her kids Roller Blade to the Circle K for snacks after school—even if there's no sidewalk and all the crossing guards have gone home.

Everyone Else's Mom buys all the "in" clothes and lets her kids wear them whenever they want to. If they get stained with spaghetti sauce or ripped in the back yard, she is happy to replace them. She gives her kids gum on the way to school if they have forgotten to brush their teeth, then reminds them to swallow it before they walk into class.

> Everyone Else's Mom doesn't care if her kids comb their hair or wear belts to hold up their pants.

She finds time to make all the beds by herself, pick up the dirty clothes, take out the garbage, and feed the animals. She is happy to do all these chores so that her kids can relax and watch TV after a long day at school. She think it's important for her kids to talk on the phone to their friends for hours, even if they have just spent the whole day together. I'm sure she has already installed a separate phone line for her children, so they will have ample opportunity to develop adequate social and communication skills.

Everyone Else's Mom never cooks vegetables, always doles out change for soda machines, and even enjoys a little MTV. I've tried for several years to meet this famous lady, but she's awfully hard to pin down. When I ask my children where she lives, they tell me she's at Michael's house, or maybe Jason's, or David's for sure. But if I get around to calling their homes, I am informed that no such lady exists at that address. She quickly disappears, only to reappear at another friend's house—one I don't know quite so well.

I figure that Everyone Else's Mom must flit from house to house lending a "hip" hand or piece of advice. What a woman! I wish she'd show up at my house once in a while just to help with the laundry! Until she does, I guess my kids will just have to fold their own clothes.

Mama Is a SCREAMER

Mark Lowry

Do you know what a SCREAMER is?

A SCREAMER is someone you don't pay any attention to—that is, until she hits a certain pitch. And you know she's hit that certain pitch when garage doors fly open all over the neighborhood.

She used to look at me and say, "MARK! You just wait till your dad comes home!"

My dad *always* came home.

He'd walk through the front door from work, and the first thing he'd hear is my mother screaming:

"CHARLES, YOU'VE GOT TO TALK TO MARK!"

I remember one time when I was eight and my brother was ten; I was in the kitchen minding my own business. My brother

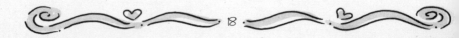

Mike, Mr. Perfect, came walking through the kitchen with that look on his face.

Have you ever seen anyone with that look? It's a look that says, "I need to be slapped."

So what was I to do? I walked over and slapped him.

The next thing I knew, I was on the floor wrestling with Mr. Perfect. He had me by the throat; I was pounding him in the face. We were having a wonderful time.

That is, until Mama had enough.

She said that a lot.

"MARK, I'VE JUST ABOUT HAD ENOUGH."

I'd say, "Well, Mama, help yourself, there's plenty more."

There came a day when I got too big to whip. By the time I was fifteen, she'd be spanking me on the rear end, and I'd be looking at my watch. Or I'd say, "Ooh, a little more to the left."

Mama didn't like that.

But I wasn't too big to spank this particular day. And while we were having a great time knocking over kitchen chairs and bouncing off the kitchen table, Mama was in the kitchen, too, washing dishes. We hardly knew she was there.

Until, that is, Mama had enough.

I wish that God would build on the back of every mother's head a little red light that would start flashing ten seconds before "enough." You can make a lot of tracks in ten seconds.

But we got no warning that morning. And before we knew what happened, Mama had thrown herself over the kitchen sink, and this is what we heard:

"I'VE FAILED! I'VE FAILED! I'VE FAILED! LORD, FORGIVE ME FOR FAILING WITH THESE BOYS!"

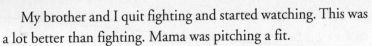
My brother and I quit fighting and started watching. This was a lot better than fighting. Mama was pitching a fit.

"I'VE FAILED! I'VE FAILED!" she kept wailing, tears splashing off her cheeks.

Then, all of a sudden, the phone started ringing.

My brother and I stared at the phone then back at Mama. Then at the phone and back at Mama.

But she didn't even let up.

"I'VE FAILED! I HAVE FAILED!" she kept screeching.

I remember thinking, "I wonder who's going to get the phone? It sure wasn't going to be my brother or me."

And that left Mama. And she sure was in no condition to answer the phone. Her eyes were all red and puffy, tears were pouring down her face, and nothing but big, wailing sobs were coming out of her mouth.

"I went through the VALLEY OF THE SHADOW OF DEATH to give you birth!"

Yet without slowing up a lick on the wailing, she turned and started walking toward the ringing phone.

I immediately started fasting and praying.

"Oh, Dear God, please don't let that be Daddy on the phone. God, I'll go to Africa, I'll wear polyester Bermuda shorts for the rest of my life. God, I'll marry a woman with a monkey on her head. Don't let that be Daddy on the phone."

Mama, still walking toward that phone, had moved into Phase Two.

"I can't BELIEVE the way you boys TREAT me (sob, honk, sniffle)!" Mama screeched as she raised her arm to the phone.

"I went through the VALLEY OF THE SHADOW OF DEATH to give you birth!" Mama bawled as she gripped the phone's receiver.

"Between the TWO OF YOU, I've been in LABOR HALF MY LIFE (honk, sniffle)!" Mama whined as she lifted the receiver from its cradle. "PUSH is more than just a sign on a door for ME!"

But then, just as the receiver got to her ear—

"And you TREAT ME (sob) LIKE...!"

Mama's voice suddenly turned peaches and cream and sweet birds singing: "Hellllooooooooooo?"

I still can't figure out how she did that.

Minivacations Even a Travel Agent Could Love

Karen Scalf Linamen

How do you know whether or not you need a vacation? In case you aren't quite sure, I've compiled a list designed to help you determine whether you should (a) arrange some time to get away from it all, or (b) go on running yourself into the ground.

If you find yourself exhibiting any number of the following symptoms, then this chapter is definitely for you.

So here they are, nine signs that you need a vacation:

1. If you find yourself looking forward to your next dentist appointment as a chance to sit and relax for a half hour...

2. If your need for Rolaids is exceeded only by your craving for chocolate...

3. If the nervous tic in your eye prompts strange men to wink back and ask you for your phone number...then you might be in need of a vacation.

4. If the music you listened to on your last getaway was Barry Manilow—on eight-track...

5. If you'd love for Calgon to take you away, but the piles of laundry in the hallway keep blocking you from getting into your bathroom...

6. If your husband is beginning to fear that the P in PMS just might stand for permanent...then there's a good chance that you're in need of a vacation.

7. If the last time you got away for dinner and a movie, you thought John Travolta looked pretty good in those white pants...

8. If the closest you've come to a vacation in the past six months has been cruising the information highway...

9. If your days are so full you can't even find time to wash your hair and shave your legs during the same shower... then there's no question. You definitely need a vacation.

3

don't laugh at me because i'm beautiful

Deep Enough
—JEAN KERR

I'm tired of all this nonsense about beauty
being only skin deep. That's deep enough.
What do you want—an adorable pancreas?

Even These Hairs Are Numbered

Sheri Rose Shepherd

I come from a long line of hair-obsessed people, and I feel secure in saying I will be continuing the tradition.

I have indelible memories of my father standing in front of the mirror with his special brush and blow dryer and a can of hair spray. He had (and still has) basically four tufts of hair, which he sculpted individually for an hour at a time. If he couldn't get his four patches of hair to lie down straight, he wouldn't leave the house. I remember him canceling business meetings at the office because his hair would not cooperate.

On bad hair days he would scream and yell and run around the house. On good hair days he enjoyed having an audience as he arranged the *coiffure du jour*, and he would sometimes make us kids get out of bed, sit in the bathroom, and watch him blow-dry his hair.

Growing up with such an example, I became a sucker for every shampoo, conditioner, treatment, and hair gimmick on TV. Several years ago I saw a commercial for clip-on hair extensions. What a great concept! You take these pieces of fake hair and clip them into your own hair for a fuller, thicker look in minutes. If Farrah Fawcett could do it, why couldn't I?

I had a big Christmas presentation to make in Arkansas, so in time for the trip I bought a pair of these clip-on hair pieces to get the thick, luxurious hair I had always dreamed about. Not one to be burdened by unnecessary instructions, I put them on having no idea how they worked. I spoke on Friday night and everything went great. My new, lush locks framed my face just so.

When I went to the podium for the final conference session on Saturday night, the lady who introduced me gave me a big old bear hug. *These people are so sweet,* I thought. I continued walking toward the microphone unaware that her embrace had unclipped one of my spiffy new hair extensions. Beginning my remarks, I couldn't help noticing that my audience seemed preoccupied. Tanna, my manager, kept pointing to her ear. I thought she needed a Q-tip or something.

> My manager kept pointing to her ear. I thought she needed a Q-tip or something.

It wasn't until I finished and sat down that I discovered that half of my lush locks were cascading down the back of my jacket and sticking out under my armpit. I looked like I was carrying a ferret. It is a testament to the power of God's message that I didn't get laughed off the stage. Despite the distraction, we actually felt a tremendous sense of outreach that weekend and saw many people give their lives to Christ.

The hair obsession that so absorbed both my father and me really served no purpose that weekend in Arkansas, or any other time in my life. If you think about it, there are probably things in your own life that don't matter, yet they have become or are becoming an obsession. They drain your energy from more productive tasks and distract you from doing God's work. I challenge you today to search yourself and ask if there's an obsession in your life that's greater than serving and loving the Lord. Let's run the race unencumbered.

Aromatherapy Overdose
Renae Bottom

If one more fruit-scented body care product hits the shelves, you can chalk me up as the first recorded victim of aromatherapy overdose.

I'm all for reviving the influence of nature in beauty care, but fruit scents have overrun the marketplace. My daily hygiene routine reads like the tutti-frutti menu at the health food store.

By the time I suds my hair with green apple shampoo, lather up with strawberry body wash, scrub my knees with apricot buffing cream, apply cranberry hand lotion, and spritz on peach body mist, I smell like a bad accident at the Farmer's Market.

Some mornings, I'm not sure if I should anchor my "do" with hair spray or Sure-Jell. If I get carried away and pop in some watermelon bubble gum on the drive to work, I run the risk of a bona fide fruit explosion.

Exuding the aroma of a walking orchard is disturbing my psyche. I'm afraid to stay out in the sun too long, lest I spoil. I linger near the produce aisle at the grocery store. If I feel overheated, I open the refrigerator and stare longingly into the crisper pan.

Late at night, I find myself rooting for the villains in "Attack of the Killer Tomatoes." I'm paranoid about bruising; I'm happiest when my skin is firm and waxy; I calculate everything in bushels.

I fantasize about spending my free time perched in the bough of a leafy tree. I've developed an unnatural fear of melon-ballers.

I've noticed that the ever-present aroma of fruit has a subliminal effect on the psyche of those around me, as well. People standing near me in a line suddenly experience an inexplicable craving for kiwi or cantaloupe. Those downwind from my position find their mouths watering for a good bunch of grapes.

My daily hygiene routine reads like the tutti-frutti menu at the health food store.

A few who suspect that the smell comes from my direction wonder why I've started bathing in apple juice. Others surmise that I've stuffed an entire package of Fruit Stripe gum in my mouth.

Believe it or not, these fruit-scented beauty products make me long for the days of musk oil. Sure, everybody in the 1970s smelled the same, but the fragrance defined a decade and it certainly cut down on fruit flies.

About the time that cinnamon and vanilla scents became popular, fragrance marketing moved into the kitchen. From the

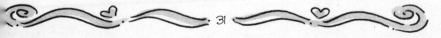

spice rack, it was a short hop to the fruit bin. Now everything we plaster on our bodies comes in citrus or seedless, take your pick. Literally.

One morning, I'll probably awaken to find that I've set on blossoms. Until then, if I'm ever discovered passed out in my bathroom, you can bet there was a sudden temperature inversion in the shower and I was overcome by the combined scents of my fruity beauty products.

I hope I can get them all used up before I go to seed. If I can, there will be no more trips to the aromatherapy aisle for me. I'm staying out of the department stores and getting my fruit fix from the grocer.

Held Hostage
in the Dressing Room
Charlene Ann Baumbich

If the sales lady told me one more time that the outfit I was viewing in the three-way mirror was "certainly body-friendly," I was going to rip the velcroed shoulder pads out of the "body-friendly" outfit and politely stuff them in her "access ready" mouth.

On the surface the phrase seemed harmless enough. After all, she was just trying to be polite. It was her way of saying that the black, flowing material covered the mid-life marks of a few too many chips and dips. But after hearing the phrase ten times in three outfits, I had heard it nine times too many. Especially after flipping the "body-friendly" price tag over and realizing that it cost even more than that bottle of anti-aging creme I purchased in a moment of insecurity and financial irresponsibility. And I wasn't about to make that mistake again!

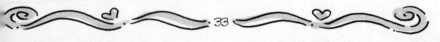

I rehashed the episode with a friend, and we decided that sales people attend seminars that teach them appropriate and tactful language.

"Forgiving" is another word sales people use to describe an outfit's camouflaging abilities. Yes, there must be workshops on how to plump up a dress while the customer stands in front of the mirror believing she is witnessing a body-shrinking miracle.

You know what I mean. You come out of the dressing room looking drab and lumpy, wearing a sad, hopeless expression, and the sales person, in a flurry of motion, adds yet another set of shoulder pads, rolls or pushes up the sleeves, blouses the material at the waistline, stands the collar up, and *voila!* You seem to have shrunk.

> We decided that sales people attend seminars that teach them appropriate and tactful language.

It perks up my ego for a fraction of a second until I remember, *you were not born with the body-shrinking talent, Charlene. You were simply born with the plump part of it.*

Do you remember the one-piece, straight-up-and-down dress that hangs in your closet like an overcooked rigatoni noodle because that's exactly how it looked on your body once you brought it home—without the sales lady? The miracle worker who whipped into your dressing room armed with a "faaaabulous" belt, a scarf, and a couple tricky ways to tie it? Those perfect accessories you didn't buy because you were sure you had something in your wardrobe bag of tricks that would pull off the same effect.

Wrong. No, I'm not falling into that trap again; I'm going to try on outfits until I find one that sings in a key that comes naturally. Not one where I have to reach falsetto pitches to wear in comfort.

And so I slip into, pull on, tug up and, in general, hurl around the dressing room until I just can't take it any longer, and, once again, come home empty-handed. Or, worse yet, with something that I settle for. Something that the sales person brought me in "another" size, a "more appropriate size in that garment, which is obviously cut on the conservative side." Something I get home and don't like as well as the "body-friendly" number I opted against in a self-righteous huff.

As I sit staring at the new outfit unbagged and draped across the living room couch—noticing the color isn't what it appeared to be under the fluorescent lights in the dressing room—I ponder the possible error in my judgment. Perhaps that annoying sales lady wasn't so bad after all. Maybe I was just in a rotten mood. Maybe I should choke down my pride and take this blah-looking specimen back. Trade it in for the black flowing thing. After all, considering that I've been gaining weight steadily for the last several over-forty years, I don't own that many clothes that fit the way they used to. Appropriate things. Things that are forgiving. Things that are, shall we say, body-friendly.

4

ten laughs, no weighting

Diet Definition
—FROM LOWELL D. STREIKER'S
A TREASURY OF HUMOR

Diet: A short period of starvation preceding a gain of five pounds.

11 Tips to Survive Swimsuit Shopping

Lynn Bowen Walker

1. Begin fasting as soon as you set your shopping date.

2. Select store based on dimness of lighting.

3. Get a pregnant friend to accompany you.

4. Check for suits tagged with bust-enhancing, waist-nipping, thigh-slimming features. Ask salesperson to point out section with "all of the above."

5. Tell yourself it's your underwear that's making the suit look so bulky.

6. Tell yourself these are "trick mirrors." You are really much slimmer in real life.

7. Convince yourself that suits with built-in shorts are not dorky. They are chic.

8. Try on all 17 styles the store carries. Head for a dimmer store.

9. Remind yourself that round is the most aesthetically pleasing shape in nature.

10. Practice sucking in your thighs.

11. On your way home with the all-black, waist-nipping, thigh-trimming suit, celebrate by stopping at ye olde ice cream shoppe. Order the "trough." But skip the whipped cream. It is, after all, bathing suit season.

I Never Met a Cookie I Didn't Fall in Love With

Nancy Kennedy

Some people say everyone has a soul mate somewhere out there. I happen to believe we can have several. After all, I do—all of them cookies.

I have loved each and every cookie I have ever met, ever since the time I was big enough to lick the front case window at my grandmother's bakery in Los Angeles. It was there I was introduced to delicate sugar cookies with maraschino cherries in the middle, sturdy nut bars, and giant, cakelike "moon cookies" with half chocolate, half white icing. But most of all I loved the chocolate-chip cookies. With my eyes as big as my hips, I'd watch as my grandmother took racks and racks of them out of her brick oven, hot and steamy and gooey. I'd snitch a few into my pocket, stuff a few in my mouth, and pile a bunch into a pink cookie box to take home with me.

Up until now, my undying devotion to cookies, especially chocolate-chip cookies, has known no end. *Give me Mrs. Fields's Chocolate Chunk Macadamia Nut cookies, or give me death!* (And give me a bigger pair of pants while you're at it.)

Therein lies the problem. As much as I love and adore cookies, which have reciprocated by attaching themselves permanently to my thighs, I'm afraid I've become, um, too big for my britches. The bod isn't what she used to be.

Now, I've been on hundreds of diets in my lifetime, and I've lost hundreds of pounds. Unfortunately I've also found them all—plus their relatives and friends—and if you ask me, it's getting too crowded in my clothes for all of us. Let's just say it's a strain, especially in the seams of my pants.

The other day I reached a breaking point. Actually it was the zipper of my jeans that reached the breaking point. I knew it was time. Despite our four-decade-long love affair, my beloved cookies had become the bane of my existence. It was time for us to part company and go our separate ways.

> I prayed that the Lord would help me slay this Cookie Monster.

Sadly, forlornly, I bid them adieu and turned to my bag of mini carrot sticks for solace. However, my heart still yearned for the silky decadence of a chocolate morsel surrounded by buttery crunchiness. *A crumb, just a crumb.* I flipped through the pages of a magazine, fantasizing over the full-color photos of holiday cookies and remembering only the day before when I had eaten my last one (double chocolate mint chunk).

I closed the magazine and prayed, "Lord, lead me not into temptation. My spirit is willing, but this body of mine is so weak!"

My craving subsided for all of three minutes; then it returned. I kept repeating, "It's not a sin to be tempted," as I opened the magazine again and started reading some recipes, waiting for God to give me strength, power, and self-control as he led me not into cookie's snare. "It's not a sin to be tempted, it's not a sin to be tempted," I chanted as I sneaked a peek at the recipe for peanut-butter jumbles. *Mmmm, peanut-butter jumbles. Peanut-butter jumbles with chocolate chips. Mmmm.*

I closed my eyes and pictured a chocolate-chip peanut-butter jumble. I imagined the aroma and did my best to recall how it might taste, the whole time congratulating myself on not falling into temptation. Instead of being filled with cookies, I was filled with self-satisfaction. I felt invincible! I was going to beat this hold that cookies had on me—and lose a few pounds in the process.

The next few days were repeats of that first. In the morning I prayed that the Lord would help me slay this Cookie Monster. Then I spent the rest of the day fighting temptation by studying magazines and cookbook recipes—yet I didn't eat a single cookie (although I did sniff the magazine picture of the blonde brownie bars and lick a bit of brown sugar off the page of the cookbook).

Then came the big test—the Cookie Exchange.

I'd been invited to my friend's cookie party and had looked forward to it for weeks. However, things had changed. Wisdom told me if I didn't go, I could avoid the temptation to eat every cookie in sight, but the more I thought about it, the more sense it made that I should go. That it was *good* for me to go, to look temptation square in the eye and say, "Ha! Gimme your best shot—I'm ready for ya." Yes, I'd prayed for God to "lead me not," but I was confident that he would not let me be tempted beyond what I could bear, and that he would provide a way of escape so I could stand up under it (1 Corinthians 10:13). I actually owed it to him to prove himself God over my temptation.

Now, despite what some people might say, I'm not a complete idiot. I knew better than to make a batch of cookies from scratch to bring with me. I'd never hold up under that kind of overwhelming temptation. Instead I decided to buy a package of cookies from the market shelf. Factory-sealed for my protection.

A funny thing happened on my way into the store. I had every intention of going right to the packaged cookie aisle, but my shopping cart took a detour to the refrigerator section where they keep the tubes of cookie dough.

Don't go there, warned the Voice inside my head.

I told the Voice, *But I'm just going to look!* And that's all I did. I looked…then ran my fingers down the seam of the package… then read the list of ingredients…then closed my eyes and tried to imagine the texture of raw dough in my mouth and the degree of bittersweetness in the chocolate chunks. *It's not a sin to be tempted,* I informed the Voice (before it had a chance to tell me I should drop everything and run).

Thoughts of hot, chewy, gooey cookies, fresh from the oven—for my friends, of course—baked into my mind. *Just think how delighted everyone will be. I owe it to them. Anyone could buy a package of cookies. These would be almost like homemade. Besides, I don't have to eat any. This is strictly an altruistic gesture. I'm doing it for others.*

Up to my elbows in thoughtfulness, I set out to bake. And just in case temptation should try to entice me, I prayed twice for the Lord to lead me not.

The first batch went in the oven without my tasting even one tiny bit. Unless you count the blob of dough that fell on the counter and the chocolate chunk that stuck to the spoon. But everyone knows that doesn't count. Neither do broken cookies (I had to eat three of those), nor burnt ones (two). Plus, as the conscientious friend that I am, I was practically *required* to sample a whole one to make sure they were edible for my friends. That left six cookies out of twelve.

The next batch I dropped on the floor. I *had* to eat those (after I brushed them off) because we have a terrible problem with ants, and I couldn't throw them in the trash.

The last batch produced six picture-perfect cookies. And four lopsided ones, which everyone knows don't count either, so I ate them as well. The rest of the dough somehow ended up in my mouth, and it wasn't until I'd eaten it that I realized...well, that I'd eaten it. But accidental eating doesn't count as "real" eating anyway. In fact, none of my cookie eating qualified as real eating, so technically I didn't succumb to temptation.

Still, I only had thirteen cookies to bring to the Cookie Exchange, and I needed three dozen. By then I didn't have time to bake any more, even if I'd had another tube of dough. I only had enough time to change into a pair of drawstring pants, finish off the remaining cookies (because of the ant problem) and stop by the store for a package of cookies.

Accidental eating doesn't count as "real" eating anyway.

On the way to the cookie exchange, I once again prayed for God to "lead me not into temptation." I planned to sip ice water all night and simply enjoy the fellowship—and leave without a plate of cookies. No one would know about my little "episode." Besides, I could always start clean tomorrow.

The first part of the evening went without a hitch. I found a spot near the table with all the cookies on it. It was far enough away that I couldn't touch them, but close enough for me to smell them. Although I'd eaten enough cookies earlier to satisfy the sweet tooth of every past, present, and future human being on earth, I didn't want to miss anything new. *What if someone brought Russian tea cakes? I'd never forgive myself for not getting a taste of those.*

Several times during the evening friends tried getting me away from my seat to join the party, but it was as if nothing else existed except cookies, glorious cookies. Eventually I did move. Closer to the table (so I could rest my water glass). I sniffed; I imagined; I savored; I salivated. I named each cookie. Blessed them. Praised them. *But I did not eat them.*

> *What if someone brought Russian tea cakes? I'd never forgive myself for not getting a taste of those.*

When everyone had divided the cookies and I had filled the tin I brought (for my family, of course), I said good night and got into my car to return home, duly impressed with myself. I opened the tin of cookies and popped one into my mouth as a congratulatory token.

That's when the Voice inside my head spoke once again. *What are you doing, Child?*

"Mmmif? Mmmif doeffn't count—I'm in ffuh car."

Suddenly the food in my mouth didn't taste as good as it had a minute ago. I swallowed what seemed like a rock. "But eating cookies isn't a sin!" I cried.

Whether you eat or don't eat cookies isn't the issue. Your flagrant flirting with the very thing you asked me to help you avoid is what concerns me. Don't you know by now that when you flirt with temptation you flirt with death?

"Death by cookies?"

Death by sin, Child. The cookies aren't important, but your soul is.

The Voice, of course, was right. I started to say, "Then why did you tempt me?" but then I remembered the words of James: "God is impervious to evil, and puts evil in no one's way. The temptation to give in to evil comes from us and only us. We have no one to blame but the leering, seducing flare-up of our own lust. Lust gets pregnant, and has a baby: sin! Sin grows up to adulthood, and becomes a real killer" (James 1:13–15 MSG).

Whether it's the temptation to eat too many cookies, spend money recklessly, watch trashy talk shows, gossip, lie, or think about men other than my husband, God never brings about the temptation, but always, always, *always* provides a way out. However, he expects me to make use of it. He's not a magic genie; he's holy God.

By the time I arrived home that night, my cookie binge had taken its toll on me. I rolled out of the car with the mother of all bellyaches and staggered to my front door. "Don't let them serve cookies at my funeral," I gasped to my husband as I crawled past him in the hall on my way to my (death) bed.

I can't be certain, but I think I heard God chuckle that night as I drifted off to sleep. I think he said something about making

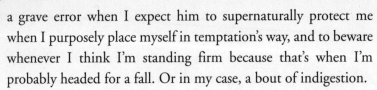

a grave error when I expect him to supernaturally protect me when I purposely place myself in temptation's way, and to beware whenever I think I'm standing firm because that's when I'm probably headed for a fall. Or in my case, a bout of indigestion.

As far as cookies being my soul mate, I've reconsidered. I think I'll get a cat instead.

Be a Loser

Karen Scalf Linamen

Recently I joined a new gym. It's great, but I have one complaint. At my old gym, the scale was located in the women's locker room. At my new gym, the scale is right next to the front desk.

You know what this means, don't you? I can no longer engage in my normal pre-weighing ritual. I can no longer lighten my load by removing my shoes, socks, leggings, T-shirt, bra, panties, wedding ring, and all of my eye makeup before stepping onto the scale. It means I gain five pounds right off the bat.

I've always hated numbers—we've never had a good working relationship. Sometimes I think there's a conspiracy and that most of the numbers in my life are out to get me. This would include not only the numbers in my checkbook but the numbers on most watches and clocks as well.

But the ringleaders have got to be the numbers on my scale. They seem to have mean-spirited agendas all their own, especially that digit in the middle. The numbers on either side are okay—they can stay. It's that middle guy who is not only malicious, but stubborn to boot.

And of course, all three numbers are celebrating as we speak, because at my new gym they get to broadcast their mean-spirited agenda in a public setting. Just last week, for example, I was stepping off the scale when I commented to a woman standing nearby, "Not exactly the best news I've had all day!" She patted my arm. "Cheer up! At least your weight is lower than mine!"

As I was walking away the implication of her words began to dawn on me. How did she know my weight was lower than hers? She peeked! I can't blame her, though—how could she have done otherwise? It's hard to be discreet with my numbers celebrating maliciously the way they always do, with party favors and bottle rockets and raucous victory dances around the face of the scale.

Of course, there's always one solution. If I want to be able to go to my new gym, approach the front desk, and weigh myself without anyone taking notice of my weight, I can always resume my pre-weighing ritual.

A naked woman may not be discreet, but at least no one will be looking at the numbers on the scale.

parenting—
not for the
faint of heart or the
slow to laugh

Mimic over Manners
—Anonymous

Children are natural mimics who act like their parents despite every effort to teach them good manners.

You Know Your Kids Are Growing Up When...

Lynn Bowen Walker

Some wise soul said the days with preschoolers drag by, but the years fly by. Boy, how they flew by. My husband and I know our sons are growing up because:

- We haven't been to the emergency room for four months.

- Our boys say please and thank you without being reminded.

- They almost always flush.

- We can take a shower in privacy from beginning to end. With our sons in the house. Awake.

- They remind us when it's time to pray.

- They want to hear stories about when they were "little."

- They can keep a secret when Daddy probes, "What did you get me for my birthday?"

- We can schedule family portraits to be taken without having to work around the facial scabs our boys used to regularly inflict on one another. (Calling each other "dummy head" has, for the time being, replaced the clawing exercises.)

- They wait for a pause in our conversation before interjecting some salient point. ("Mom, do spiders have six or eight legs?")

- Their night light burned out and they haven't asked for a replacement.

- They telephone their friends and do more than just breathe.

- We find "God Loves You" notes in little boys' handwriting, and we hear voices singing "Jesus, Name above All Names" from the next room.

We realize that, though our work is not yet done, by God's grace much has already been accomplished. And all we can do is sit back and marvel.

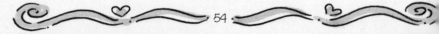

All Mama Ever Wanted

Mark Lowry

When I was a kid, I got a lot of spankings. These days, there is a big controversy about whether or not kids should be spanked. Well, that controversy is about thirty years too late, because my dad never heard it.

When I was growing up, most of my spankings were because of—I know this is going to be hard for you to believe—my mouth.

I can hear your gasp of shock.

My mouth's main problem was sassing my mother.

We'd start off with a disagreement, it would move on to an argument, and then it would end up with me sassing her.

I could never pass up a good line.

And at that point in the discussion, Mama would always tell me what she wanted out of life.

Every time. Every day. Probably two or three times a day. She would say the same thing.

At the same point in our argument, at the moment my mouth would sass her, she'd tell me the only thing she truly wanted.

Mama didn't care about new houses. She didn't care about new cars or new clothes. She had everything but the one thing she wanted most.

All my mother wanted out of life was "The Last Word."

She'd say, "Mark, you had BETTER let me have the LAST WORD."

. . . ♡ . . .
If the preacher
was going to wash
the windows on
Thursday night,
we filled our pew
and we watched
him do it.
. . . .

And to be fair, I tried to give her the last word. But something brilliant would always pop into my mind and be out of my mouth before I could stop it.

So since I never gave her that last word, I got those whippings.

The last whipping I got was when I was fifteen. I was skinny back then. I had acne. I was like a pimple-cream poster child. I had braces on my teeth before they were fashionable. My brother accused me of eating car antennas.

And I had grown too big for Mama.

It all began on the way to school one morning, when I sassed Mama.

I don't remember what it was about. But I know how it ended: "MARK, I'm going to tell your FATHER."

I was thinking, "Yeah, right. She'll forget."

She didn't.

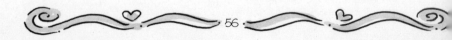

I went on to school. That afternoon, I went to Driver's Ed. After Driver's Education, my dad would always pick me up. And naturally, I would ask, "Can I drive to church?" Because we were always on our way to church. And this happened on a Wednesday. We were Baptists, and good Baptists went to Wednesday night prayer meeting. When the church doors were open, we were there. Daddy was a dictator. We did not have a vote every four years on who was gonna run the family. Daddy ran the family, and we went to church. If the preacher was going to wash the windows on Thursday night, we filled our pew and we watched him do it.

And don't think I didn't try to get out of going to church, like any normal kid. Many times, I'd say, "Daddy, I'm too sick to go to church."

He'd say, "Throw up and prove it."

And if I couldn't throw up, I went to church.

And if I DID throw up, he'd say, "Now don't you feel better? Let's go to church."

And that is a very important part of this story, because I came out of Driver's Education thinking we were going to church like we had done for the past fifteen years I had been in that family.

I walked up to our car, and said, "Daddy, can I drive to…?"

"Get in the car," he said, cutting me off.

And it was his God-voice:

GET IN THE CAR.

All of a sudden, I remembered what I had done. I started praying: "Oh, Lord Jesus, come quickly."

I got in the car. And Daddy said, "Mark, do you remember sassing your Mother this morning?"

"Yes sir."

"We're not going to church. I'm going to take you home and I'm going to half-kill you."

Have you ever been half-killed?

I started thinking, "What am I going to do? If we're skipping church to give me a whipping, it's going to be a DOOZY!"

For the whole thirty-minute drive home, I was desperately thinking, "What am I going to do? What am I going to do!"

And then a thought dawned on me. A college student had told me once, "Mark, the next time you get a spanking, try 'mind over matter.' I learned it in college. Get a blanket and bite it. Bite the blanket. Concentrate on the blanket. And you won't even feel what your dad's doing down south."

When I was fifteen, I thought all college students were brilliant. Now I'm here to tell you, they ain't. This college girl was about three fries short of a Happy Meal, if you ask me.

Because my daddy didn't whip you anywhere near where you'd bite a blanket.

When we got home, Daddy said what he always said:

"Go upstairs and prepare for your spanking."

I still don't have any idea what that means.

That started with my older brother. When he got a spanking, he would go upstairs and he would prepare. He knew what it meant: Go into your room, cry, think about what you've done, ask God to forgive you, and try to figure out how you'll never do that again.

Nobody ever explained that to me. So I would always go up and prepare.

I'd put on seventeen pairs of underwear and pull my jeans

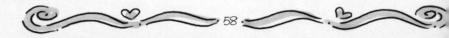

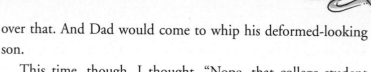

over that. And Dad would come to whip his deformed-looking son.

This time, though, I thought, "Nope, that college student told me to bite the blanket, so that's what I'm gonna do."

I went upstairs, and for thirty minutes I crammed this fuzzy University of Houston blanket down my throat. Most of that blanket was in my digestive tract before Dad entered my room. The spread was hanging out of my mouth. I was into that blanket. Or, I should say, it was into me. If I was going to try mind over matter, I was going to do it right.

I heard Daddy coming up the steps.

It sounded like this:

Boom! Boom! Boom! Click! And C-R-E-E-E-A—A-K! (We've got big doors in Texas.)

Daddy walked over to me and said, "Mark, this is going to hurt me worse than it hurts you, son."

"Go upstairs and prepare for your spanking."

Every time he said it, I would think, "Well, if that's the case, let's trade places. I'm the one who needs the punishment, so let me beat the tar out of you for once." But I never said it.

And then I heard the sound that, to this day, puts goosebumps up and down my spine. You know the sound? It's the sound of a belt flying from your daddy's beltloops.

Bp-bp-bp-bp-bp-bp-bp. POW!

You hear that, and you know Judgment Time has come.

The worst part of that night's whipping wasn't the whipping. It was the advice that college student gave me. For three days, I coughed up furballs and picked fuzz out of my braces.

But I've got a plan. I can't wait until Mom and Dad come to live with me. Oh, what a day that will be! The day Mama moves in with me, I'm taking the car keys away from her. She'll say, "Well, Scott Davis lets his mother drive."

I'm going to look at her and say, "But I'm not Scott Davis. Now go clean up your room. It's a pig sty in there, young lady. Don't start crying or I'll give you something to cry about."

Missing the Manual

Gwendolyn Mitchell Diaz

I have always thought that children should come into this world with instruction manuals attached to them. Dishwashers and lawn mowers do. Their manuals not only list all the parts involved and how to keep them functioning smoothly, but they tell you what to do when something goes wrong. There's a technical support number to call for advice if things get really bad, and, if all else fails, you can just package up the product and return it to the manufacturer!

Shouldn't kids come with such information and guarantees?

Sure, the pediatrician gives you a list of shots as you leave the hospital. The nurse hands you a pamphlet telling you when to start feeding the infant oatmeal and what to do the first time your child catches a cold or swallows a marble. La Leché even

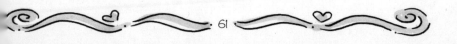

offers a toll-free number for advice, but it deals with only one area of childrearing.

I'm quite aware that the library has all kinds of reference books outlining the developmental stages of life, and I've seen umpteen books explaining exactly how to potty train a strong-willed child. I realize many great books have been written on how to raise emotionally and spiritually healthy children. But what I need is a manual stocked with a few more of the practical facts of childrearing—hard, cold facts on how to get them through the intricacies of everyday life.

> I want a list of science fair projects that are guaranteed to take no more than three hours of my time.

I want to be given a list of science fair projects that are guaranteed to take no more than three hours of my time and can still get my child (at least) a "B."

I want a book that will contain practical ideas on how to build a functional family dwelling. It should make suggestions such as: "Houses built for the purpose of raising kids must be constructed with at least one solid cement wall containing no windows or doors. Such a wall will become the focal point for neighborhood play. It is guaranteed to supply hours of free fun without the additional cost of broken windows."

I want to be warned that every neighbor who buys cheese-and-cracker fund-raisers from my kids will expect me to buy wrapping-paper products from theirs. Someone should inform parents that it would be cheaper and smarter to donate twenty bucks to the school up front and avoid the hassle of collecting money and distributing cheese balls that nobody really wants and nobody will ever eat!

I would like to know early on in the child-raising process that simple things like flashlights and measuring tapes can fascinate kids for hours, and that a hammer and nails will get a lot more use than an expensive video game.

I would like to know what the phone-calling rules are. Is it really okay for girls to call boys these days? If so, does that just include homework calls, or is it acceptable for the girls to arrange for dates and ask boys to the prom?

I would also like some pointers on how to keep my cool when my fifteen-year-old son announces that he is going to the big city on Friday night with his buddies, and I find out that the guy who will be driving just passed his driver's exam—the day before.

Yes, I think *The Complete Book on Raising Kids* would come in very handy. Unfortunately, most of us would probably ignore such an instruction manual (just like we ignored the one that came with the bicycle), until we messed things up so badly they couldn't be salvaged.

Others might study the manual too deeply, accepting it as the ultimate authority in childrearing. They wouldn't feel the need to turn to God with a trustful heart and a faithful smile.

I guess being stuck raising kids without a complete how-to manual is a rather compelling way for God to get us to depend on Him!

blushing beauties

—embarrassing moments

Bow Your Heads

—FROM LIVING IT DOWN BY LAUGHING IT UP
BY MARTHA BOLTON

When my son, Tony, was asked to say the prayer for the offering one night at church, he was a little nervous. He didn't admit he was, but I think it was obvious when he asked everyone to bow their heads, then proceeded to pray, "Lord, bless us as we bring you our thighs."

Yuk It Up!
Patsy Clairmont

We all have moments we'd rather not remember—the kind that when we do recall them, we get embarrassed all over again. Like finding you're dragging a long sweep of toilet tissue. Spike heels are great for that. You shish kebab the tissue on your way out of the restroom, and you can literally parade it for miles before anyone will tell you.

Having dragged my pantyhose behind me through my hometown has left me with empathy for other dragees. I remember a gentleman and his wife who approached me at a convention and related their adventure.

The man said, "If you think it's embarrassing for a woman to drag her pantyhose, how do you think a man feels when it happens to him? I went to work and walked through the office when

one of the women sang out, 'What's that, Bill?' I turned to look, and dangling out of my suit-pants leg were my wife's pantyhose. I casually ambled over to a wall, shook them out, and walked away. I left the hose huddled in the corner to figure out their own transportation home."

Evidently his wife didn't pick up her pantyhose, but the static in his slacks did. Half the hose clung to his pant leg, while the remaining leg danced behind him. The man, his wife, and I laughed long and loud as he relived his tale.

There's something so healing about laughter. When I can laugh at an event that has the potential to turn my pale face flashing red, somehow the situation doesn't record itself in my memory with as much pain.

My friend Ann is a good example. She flipped her melon and lived to laugh about it. While she was shopping for groceries one time, she spotted a large, elongated watermelon. She wanted the melon, but it looked heavy, and she wasn't sure she could lift it. No stock boys were around, so she decided to give it the old heave-ho. Either the melon didn't weigh as much as she had thought, or she was stronger than she realized. Anyway, she grabbed hold of the watermelon and slung it up and toward herself. With torpedo speed, the slippery melon slid out of her hands and up her shoulder to become airborne.

> Either the melon didn't weigh as much as she had thought, or she was stronger than she realized.

Once again, Sir Newton's theory of gravitation proved true. The melon headed for earth with great rapidity. When a melon is dropped from more than five feet onto a tile floor, "splat" doesn't

begin to describe what occurs. Not only did it explode, but everything in a 15-foot radius was affected as well.

As Ann turned to look at her Herculean effort gone awry, she spotted…a victim. Or should I say the victim was "spotted"? A nicely dressed businesswoman looked stunned as ragged chunks of watermelon dripped down her pantyhose.

Ann didn't mean to laugh, but the whole scene struck her as so absurd that she couldn't help herself. The lady was not laughing, which seemed to tickle Ann all the more. The woman marched off in a huff, leaving a trail of seeds behind her.

Ann was now leaning against the rutabagas, trying to catch her breath, when the manager walked up and said, "This is not funny."

Well, that was the wrong thing to say. Poor Ann howled. Her sides were splitting, her face was red, and she was hysterical. She said she was trying to gain her composure so she could find the lady and apologize to her. But finally she had to just leave the store.

Laughter can make moments more memorable. Whether laughing alone or with others, it helps us feel good about our memories.

I remember walking through the mall once when I noticed a quarter on the floor. Had it been a penny, I might have passed it by. But a quarter? No way. I stooped down and swooped my hand across the floor to scoop up the coin, but it didn't budge. I tried again. I could hear laughter coming from a nearby ice cream shop, but I didn't look because I was focused on the shiny coin. I tried to pick it up again, but it held fast. I tried prying it with my nails. I even took out my emery board and used it like a crowbar, trying to dislodge this gleaming coin.

As I stared at George Washington's immobile silhouette, I thought I saw him smirk. Then I realized George was not alone. The laughter nearby had grown to unbridled guffawing. I looked up and realized five teenagers were watching me and laughing at my financial struggle. It was the kind of laugh that told me they knew something I didn't.

I could have flown off in a fury or resented their intrusion. Then again, I could find out what was so hilarious and join the fun.

I asked, "Okay, what's the deal?"

One girl confessed they had glued the quarter to the floor and had been watching people try to pick it up. The kids dubbed me with the "most dedicated to the task." I giggled with them as I thought about my 25-cent antics.

Laughter is an incredible gift. It helps us to not take ourselves too seriously and makes it possible for us to survive life's awkward moments.

Blinded by the Light

Sheri Rose Shepherd

Not long after I graduated from high school, I decided to enter my first beauty pageant: Miss San Jose, California. Part of every beauty pageant is "the walk." Dressed in evening gowns, the contestants parade like movie stars one at a time down a runway toward the audience. The runway and stage are lined with tiny lights, and spotlights follow each contestant as she walks down to the end of the runway, makes a turn, and walks back.

Of course, my fellow contestants and I had all practiced smiling, waving, and walking during rehearsal—and many of us had been practicing it since we were children. During the rehearsal, however, there weren't a thousand people sitting out in the audience, and the Miss San Jose crown was not actually on the line. An even bigger difference was that during the competition, the auditorium was pitch-dark, the spotlights were right in our eyes,

and we couldn't see a thing in front of us—even if the thing happened to be the judges' table.

When my turn came, I sauntered down the runway toward the light, beaming my best competition smile and doing the figure-eight wave like a pro. I took one confident step after another until, suddenly, there was nothing to step on. I went flying through space off the end of the runway and landed with an unqueenly thud—smack on top of the judges' table.

The audience gasped in unison. All was lost. But just because I was flat on my face didn't mean I couldn't be quick on my feet. Mustering my perkiest smile, I rolled off the table and hopped up on my heels. I straightened my sequins, looked up at the judges without missing a beat, and exclaimed, "I just wanted you to remember me." With that, I crawled back onto the runway and walked offstage the right way. If I was going to go down in flames, I might as well go with a little panache.

I learned a life lesson that night. It's not how I act, but how I react that makes the difference. The judges not only remembered me, they awarded me the title of Miss San Jose. My reaction had turned embarrassment into triumph—though I don't recommend it as a strategy for aspiring pageant contestants!

How many peaks and valleys could there be in one day? After my victory, my family and I all went to a Mexican restaurant to celebrate. I was starving! I hadn't eaten real food in three weeks. With admiring relatives and curious onlookers surrounding me, I lunged for the nachos. As I did, my shiny new crown slid off and scored a direct hit into the refried beans.

God never runs out of imaginative ways to keep us humble.

Sure I Can!

Patsy Clairmont

Most of us over 40 find it difficult to believe we're losing our youth. Our minds are still spunky, at least in a sputtering kind of way, and tend to send inaccurate information to our bodies like "You can still leap buildings in a single bound." Right. I can hardly step into an elevator without having my arches fall.

At 47 (at the time of this writing), my mind is marching to "The Battle Hymn of the Republic," while my body is humming in the background, "That'll Be the Day." Even with my increasing physical disruptions, I keep holding my thumb over the birth date on my driver's license when I'm cashing a check.

My friend Claris, a heroic woman who drove school buses for 19 years and has lived to tell of it, forgot her age. It had to be amnesia that caused her to be coaxed into going roller-skating in her forties. An hour later she was in an ambulance, and she wasn't

driving. A cast, crutches, and several months later, Claris was back wheeling around in her bus, which has the only size wheels she now trusts to hold her up. Speaking of holding up…

Jim was certain he could reach a little higher than his arm span while tottering on the top rung of the ladder. Need I tell you any more? Our fiftyish friend came down like the Jericho walls, but instead of broken pitchers, he had broken ribs. After being taped back together, he felt every breath he took. Speaking of breathtaking…

Meagan decided to take up downhill skiing…at 40. Her first time out she fell backward on her skis, but they didn't release. That was not good. Meagan had to be removed from the slopes on a stretcher by the ski patrol. She wore a mega foam collar for months.

You would think we would learn from our friends' examples. Well, actually I did. I didn't roller-skate, climb ladders, or ski downhill. No, not me: I'm too smart to try those tricky feats. Instead, I decided to ride a five-speed bicycle. My infamous ride would have been a cinch had I ever before ridden a bike with the brakes on the handlebars, which I had not. That became quite clear to who knows how many.

My son Jason and I rode our bikes to a nearby store, where, instead of braking when the bike slowed down, I side-saddled it and jumped off like Annie Oakley. I ran into the store and bought a couple of small items. We didn't have a basket, but I was confident I could manage the bike and the bags. It had been many years since I had ridden a bicycle. (Actually, I was eight when I got my last bike.) But you know what they say: "Once you learn, you never forget."

We were almost home when my bike began to pick up speed.

Evidently there was more of an incline on our street than I had realized. For a moment I felt like a kid again, with the wind whipping through my tresses and the houses passing by in a whirl of colors. Suddenly I recognized the whirling greens as my house. I instinctively pedaled backward to brake. Nothing happened. I mean, nothing happened! My acceleration was such that I could see I was headed rapidly for the side street. If my calculations were correct, I would cross it at the speed of light.

Feeling I was losing control of this ride, I kind of panicked. Then I recalled Les's reminding me, as I rode away, that the brakes were located on my handlebars, and that I should squeeze them to stop. I could only grip on one side because of the bag, and when I squeezed, nothing happened. Seeing my life skateboard past me, I grabbed for the other grip, bag and all, and pulled as hard as I could. Sure enough, something happened!

> *I instinctively pedaled backward to brake. Nothing happened. I mean, nothing happened!*

I became airborne. Over the handlebars and into the wild, blue yonder. I'm sure I looked like a 747 wide-body. That is, until my landing. I did a belly-flop glide down my sidewalk/ runway, stopping just before I became a permanent design on our front steps.

Jason looked down at me in utter amazement. I'm not sure if he couldn't believe I could ride a bicycle that fast or fly that high.

If this happened to you or you had observed it happening to someone else, what would you expect the first words out of the person's mouth to be? Perhaps "Call 911!" or "Get your dad!"

Well, that's what a normal person might say. But not me. The

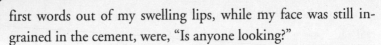

first words out of my swelling lips, while my face was still in-grained in the cement, were, "Is anyone looking?"

Is anyone looking! Give me a break! The sidewalk/slide had torn my pant leg off, my knee was ripped and gushing, I had skid marks on my stomach, my elbow felt like Rice Krispies, my ribs had a Vise-Grip on my lungs, and I wanted to know, "Is anyone looking?" With Jason's help, I limped into the house, carefully lowered myself into a chair, and cried. My tears were as much out of embarrassment as from pain.

From my emotional response, I had obviously damaged something more than my body. Mine was a giveaway statement of someone suffering from fractured pride.

But then I wondered: Isn't that true for any of us who can't ac-cept our limitations?

laughter,
family style

Dog Heaven
—MARK TWAIN

Heaven goes by favor; if it went by merit,
you would stay out and your dog would go in.

Pet Peeve
Pamela Shires Sneddon

When I was seven, I got my first pet—a little black kitten I called Tommy. Since then I have had nine kids, and an uncountable number of animals have come and mostly gone. Needless to say, the thrill has diminished a bit.

Still, I have dealt with enough pet-ownership traumas to consider myself somewhat of an expert on what parents need to know about kids and pets.

The first question is whether or not kids should even have pets. There are two sides to this issue. On one side there is the kid who wants a pet. On the other side—the mean, heartless side—we have the parents.

Often, only one parent takes the heartless side and will be referred to as Parent A. The other parent, Parent B, although an adult, should be put on the side of the kid because he or she is

either a sucker for the histrionics of a ten-year-old or susceptible to puppy dog eyes or both. Parent B can be of either sex. If Parent B is the male parent, he talks about pet ownership, teaching responsibility, or about comradeship, or stresses the usefulness of the pet. If Parent B is the female parent, she mainly talks about "those eyes!"

The pro-pet arguments voiced by the child will include solemn promises about how he or she will faithfully feed the pet, walk the pet, clean up after the pet, carry out the garbage, do the dishes, keep his or her room immaculate, eat his or her vegetables for the rest of their lives. If only they can have this wonderful, smart, no-problem pet. "Please, please, please. I promise to take care of it," is the standard phrase used by a desperate kid.

So much for a pet not being any trouble.

In order to consider the kid's argument, particularly the part about hardly-any-trouble, it might be helpful to examine a hypothetical situation. First, assume that hard-hearted Parent A has employed a typical ultimatum, in this case the "You-will-get-geese-over-my-dead-body!" ultimatum. Let's say Parent A comes home from work one day and hears mysterious peeping noises. Refusing to believe such obvious ploys as "Oh, it's probably the washer," he investigates and discovers two baby geese (technically, goslings) in a cardboard box in his daughter's bedroom. He is unable to react in the way he intended, especially in front of a freckle-faced, red-headed girl clutching two yellow, downy babies who are making adorable little whispery sounds in her hair. Is he ready to go to war over this? No, once the geese are there, there's no turning back. Surrender to the cause. Later, when they are big ganders, biting the mailman, the neighbors, dangerous to man and beast, they will have become part of the environment, entrenched forever.

Not only that, Parent A may find himself on a fine Sunday afternoon, in the middle of football season, hammering his thumb to a pulp building a goose pen or sloshing evil-smelling fluids over his good running shoes as he empties out a plastic swimming pool/goose potty. He may even find himself outside in his underwear at 1 A.M. on a moonless night, baseball bat in hand, ready to do battle against coyotes and raccoons. Notice the lack of involvement on the part of Parent B, that devious being, who instigated the whole hypothetical situation. So much for a pet not being any trouble.

For most parents, this may seem an extreme case, especially if they live in an apartment. For parents in this position, perhaps it might be better to consider a reptile. Some people might regard reptiles as cheating in the pet category. "How much trouble could a turtle be?" they ask. Obviously, they have never dealt with a turtle, especially a turtle who manages to escape an expensive glass turtle palace and wedge himself (or herself) between a wall and a dresser until—well, let's not talk about turtles.

Consider instead, snakes. In the snake category there is often a unanimous front on behalf of Parent A and Parent B: "There will be no snakes in this house!" The statement is clear. Case closed.

Meanwhile, let us suppose the kid—make that a teenage kid who announces rather than asks—has just received a pet boa constrictor from her boyfriend. In this hypothetical situation, the teenage kid swears the snake will be no trouble, that the parents will hardly know it is there. This is not reassuring. In the case of

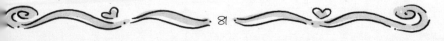

a snake, parents want to know it is there and not somewhere else, waiting for an opportunity to hunt them down and smother them in their sleep. Okay, say the snake has no interest in parents personally but just likes to slip out and roam about the house. Snakes are much better than turtles at achieving this goal.

Let's assume the snake is out of its cage doing a little reconnaissance work—for about two weeks. At this point, Parent A and Parent B assume the snake has escaped from the house and is gone forever. Chalk one up for the kid. One day, Parent B receives a phone call. Further assume it's an important call and Parent B needs to write down crucial information. There is no writing implement of any kind where Parent B answered the phone, but she remembers she found a pen last week in the living room couch. Have her maintain a professional yet pleasant tone, engaging in some light banter as she tucks the portable phone under her chin while frantically ripping up the couch cushions to find… Yes! The missing snake.

Even though we will assume the snake comes out in much better shape than Parent B or the caller's eardrums, this seems to me to disqualify the "you won't even know it is there" argument.

Perhaps it is time to consider other pro-pet assertions: A pet will teach a kid responsibility, provide companionship, and be useful. Let's look first at the idea that having a pet will teach a kid responsibility. The pet most sought after to teach responsibility is a dog. Dogs, especially puppies, are pretty much irresistible (those eyes!), even to that grouchy Parent A. The problem is that while dogs hang around for a while, a kid's responsibility packaging has a very short shelf life.

In other words, Parent B six months from now will be walking the pet, cleaning up after the pet, feeding the pet. And there is the financial side of responsibility. Can you really expect an eight-year-old to pay for the pet's shots, flea collars, thyroid blood panel, or possible emergency room visits for ingesting odd objects?

Okay, Parent B might say, maybe a kid can't be that responsible, but a pet will be a companion like Lassie, Rin-tin-tin, Beethoven, and Old Yeller. The list is endless of loyal, loving dogs who star in their own movies or television shows. Heck, even a hamster provides a kind of comradeship in between nibbling patterns in the curtains. Parent A will be hard put to come up with a sizzling retort on this one.

> A kid's
> responsibility
> packaging has a
> very short
> shelf life.

And then there is the potential usefulness of the pet. The kid and Parent B might cite numerous cases to bolster their strategy at this point: The dog that wakes up the family when the house is on fire; the dog that saves a child from a raging river; the dog that protects his master at the risk of its own life; the cat that, well, the cat that leaves the most delectable parts of a gopher on the new down comforter. (At least the rest of the gopher is no longer putting holes in the lawn.)

So, if you've been contemplating getting a family pet, these are some things to mull over: A pet will be trouble, you will know it is there, and you will be the one stuck with the pet when the kid goes off to college. Is it worth it? Well—just a minute, I have to go feed the cat, check the bird, and walk the dog. The thing is, they all had these eyes....

Honey, They Flushed the Cat

Nancy Kennedy

Barry and I were hiding—in our bedroom, away from Laura and what seemed like a thousand of her closest personal friends as they performed standard slumber-party rituals. There was The Full-Face Makeover, the "Let's Call _____ and Ask Him If He Likes You" and the "Uh-oh! Does Your Mom Get Mad If There's Salsa on the Rug?"

With two daughters, we'd done this hundreds of times before. The strange part was that after surviving Slumber Party No. 1, we continued to say yes to Parties No. 2 through 200.

"Do they have to play the CDs *and* the VCR at the same time?" asked Barry as he peeked out the bedroom door.

I smiled and patted him on the shoulder. "You've obviously never been an eighth-grade girl."

"What are they doing?" He stuck his head out further and

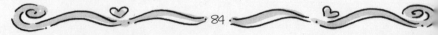

sniffed. "Chocolate." (Sniff.) "Pizza." (Sniff, sniff.) "And…come here. I can't quite make this one out."

I joined him at the door and took a whiff. "It's…it's…" I couldn't tell either. It was a cross between caramel corn, cat food and cheap perfume. "You'd better go check it out," I told him.

My husband looked at me as if I'd suggested he wax his leg hair. "But that's *your* job," he cried.

"My job? Why is it my job?"

He wrinkled his brow. "I don't know. But I'm almost positive it's in your job description."

Barry and I constantly refer to an imaginary document: the Parental Job Description Manual.

"Page 5," Barry said, "Herein, from date of child's birth, the role of mother shall include (but not be limited to) investigating odd odors coming from any and all offspring and/or their friends, pets or science projects."

> "Herein, the role of mother shall include (but not be limited to) investigating odd odors coming from any and all offspring."

"Ah," I said. "But the footnote says the mother can pass this job on to her husband at her discretion."

"Keep reading," he said. "The mother has to have a good reason to pass on this job or else the pass is null and void."

I thought for a moment. "How about this: 'If it doesn't involve blood, expensive machinery or fire we don't want to know?'"

Barry stuck his head out the bedroom door again and called to Laura. "You girls aren't using the stove or sharp knives or the dishwasher, are you?"

"No, Dad!" she called back. "We're just playing with Alex!"

We heard the toilet flush, and the cat made an uncharacteristic sound. "What does the manual say about kids dunking cats in the toilet?" he asked. It doesn't address that particular act, so Barry took charge of the investigation.

> "What does the manual say about kids dunking cats in the toilet?"

When we first married, Barry and I had grand, romantic daydreams about how we were going to raise our children. We'd see a couple pushing a stroller and one of us would start with, "When we have kids, we'll both share equally in the work. We'll take turns changing diapers and getting up in the middle of the night and fishing bugs out of their mouths. We'll both go to PTA meetings and Little League games. We'll be united in all things. Even-Steven."

But then we actually had kids. That's when we realized we each had separate and distinct parenting roles. For example, the one with the proper equipment is the one who nurses the baby. That one was a no-brainer. Here are a few other duties recorded in the Parental Job Description Manual.

- *Icky Stuff Wiper.* Generally, moms wipe noses, backsides and everything in between. It's a natural reflex evidenced by the first maternal action: a mother, upon seeing her newborn for the first time, will instinctively lick her thumb and wipe her child's cheek. In contrast, upon seeing anything gooey or slimy on his child's person, a dad will instinctively gag and say, "Go see Mommy."

- *Creepy Thing Killer.* This is typically a dad-thing. It begins at childhood (the dad's) with squishing bugs and shaking salt on unsuspecting slugs. It's the hunter-gatherer reflex and usually causes the "My hero!" response in admiring females.

- *Birthday Party Giver.* This job falls to the person who can stand to be in a room with seven sugar-shocked young-sters, all clamoring for more cake, more soda, more turns with the birthday child's toys and/or more "horsey rides" on the dog's back, and still remember which guest is aller-gic to chocolate and which one needs his or her inhaler half-way through the party.

- *Parallel Parking Instructor.* We flipped a coin when it came time to teach our daughter Alison to drive. I won. So Barry had the pleasure of having his stomach muscles tie themselves in knots as he screamed, "Turn the wheel to the left! No, your other left!" while I stayed home and took a long bath.

- *Embarrasser.* This is one job we share equally, although we each have individual means of expression for this vital parental role. While I tend more toward the "just being a mom" method of embarrassment (which includes bring-ing forgotten lunches into math class and calling teachers by their first names), Barry goes in for the more obvious horn honking when driving past You-Know-Who, or wav-ing to You-Know-Who's parents, or inviting them all over for a barbecue.

Barry interrupted my job description review when he came back to the bedroom and started looking for a ball game on TV. Laura and her throng of friends had decided not to baptize the cat and instead had turned their attention to drawing tattoos on their arms with colored markers. I shook my head and gave thanks that that's *all* they were doing.

Then I remembered we had another job to do, and we had to do it together. I reached underneath the bed and pulled out two cans of Silly String. I handed one to Barry, and we inched our way down the hall toward the living room...

Would You Like a Coronary with Your Coffee?

Karen Scalf Linamen

I have lots of stories about negotiating the strangest things with total strangers. But perhaps my favorite story is the time we nearly put my father-in-law in the hospital.

It all started when Dad, a college professor and administrator at Anderson University for more than thirty-five years, wrote us about a retirement dinner the university was hosting in his honor. Dad also wrote, "But don't come. It's too much money to fly from Texas to Indiana, and I want to spare you the time and expense."

Larry decided to surprise his father by showing up unannounced for the special event.

Suddenly I had an idea. I asked Larry, "Want to REALLY surprise your dad?"

Larry said, "How?"

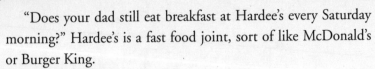

"Does your dad still eat breakfast at Hardee's every Saturday morning?" Hardee's is a fast food joint, sort of like McDonald's or Burger King.

Larry thought a minute. "I think so. Why?"

I said, "Trust me."

I got on the phone, called Hardee's, and made all the arrangements. Using my best negotiating tactics, I somehow talked the manager into letting Larry slip into a Hardee's uniform and wait behind the counter for Dad to show up for breakfast.

Larry flew into town on a Friday night and stayed with a friend. On Saturday morning he "went to work" at Hardee's. At precisely nine o'clock, my mother-in-law, father-in-law, and cousins Forry and Zula Carlson entered Hardee's. The three fellow conspirators sent Dad to the counter to order, then hung back to watch the fun.

> "How can you be out of coffee? I can see the coffeepot right behind you!"

Larry, wearing the Hardee's shirt and hat, stepped up to the counter and faced his dad. He said, "Your order, please."

Dad looked at him.

There was a long pause.

Dad said, "I'll have the breakfast burrito."

Larry said, "We're out of those."

Dad said, "In that case, I guess I'll have a sausage biscuit."

Larry said, "We're out of those, too."

Dad said, "I've never heard of such a thing! Well then, just give me a cup of coffee."

Larry said, "We're out of coffee, too."

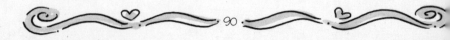

Dad's face and neck began to flush. "How can you be out of coffee? I can see the coffeepot right behind you!"

At about that time, Larry took off his paper cap and burst into laughter. "Hey, Dad, don't you recognize your own son?"

I wasn't there at the time. But I understand that what happened next was like a scene straight out of that old sitcom *Sanford and Son*, where Fred Sanford grabs his heart and staggers backwards, claiming to be heaven-bound.

'Cept Dad wasn't faking.

He didn't have a heart attack. But he staggered backwards in shock. Good thing family members were there to catch him. I probably should have negotiated some paramedics into the deal as well. My father-in-law lived to attend his retirement dinner that night, and to this day loves to tell the story of Larry's twelve-minute career as a clerk at Hardee's.

8

till death do us
laugh
—marriage humor

It Could Happen
—Anonymous

If we can put a man on the moon...why not all of them?

Fun Questions for Married Couples

Bill and Pam Farrel

Here is a little quiz to help you see how well you understand the uniqueness each of you brings to your relationship.

1. The recreational activity you most often do together is:

   A. Bicycling.

   B. Bowling.

   C. Hunting for his car keys.

2. Choose a vacation spot! Which qualifications for a prime vacation spot would appeal to the husband, and which would appeal to the wife?

   A. Quaint little shops.

B. Golf, golf, golf.

C. Nice restaurants.

D. Big servings.

E. Valet parking.

F. Free parking.

G. Room with a view.

H. Room with a television set.

I. Elegant sunken tub.

J. Reading matter in the bathroom.

3. TRUE OR FALSE: A vacuum cleaner makes an excellent anniversary gift.

   TRUE! Provided you want it to be your last anniversary.

4. STORY PROBLEM: John and Betty must leave their home by 6 P.M. in order to be on time for a dinner party. John starts to get ready at 5:55 P.M. so he can leave at 6 P.M. What time does Betty need to start getting ready in order to leave by 6 P.M.?

   ANSWER: It makes no difference when Betty starts to get ready. She could start at 5 P.M., 4 P.M., or even 3 P.M. It doesn't matter. She's still going to be at least 20 minutes late.

5. (Husband question) When your wife says, "Let's not get each other Christmas presents this year," it indicates:

A. Her desire to share with the less fortunate.

B. Her thoughtful and realistic interest in the household budget.

C. A test to see if you "love her enough" to forget the suggestion and "surprise" her with something you'll be paying off until Columbus Day.

6. When a husband dons his almost-like-new coveralls and announces, "I'm going to work on the car," you can almost bet that:

A. Soon, it will purr like a kitten.

B. Soon, it will stop on a dime.

C. Soon, it will be towed to a nearby garage.

7. (Husband question) FILL IN THE BLANK: You can't make an omelet without:

A. Breaking some eggs.

B. Reading a recipe.

C. Hearing a lecture from your wife on the dangers of cholesterol.

8. Who is more likely to utter the following:

A. "What's for supper?"
   Him   Her

B. "Have you seen my socks?"
   Him   Her

C. "When are we leaving for church?"

Him   Her

D. "Do you think I've gained weight?"

Him   Her

E. "Where's the television schedule?"

Him   Her

9. Before answering the question "How do you like my new hairstyle?" what should a husband always remember?

   A. His wife's feelings are the most important thing.

   B. She may have spent hours in a salon to get it to look that way.

   C. The couch is lumpy, and when you sleep on it a spring pokes you in the back.

10. His idea of the perfect honeymoon is:

    A. A week in the Poconos.

    B. A Mediterranean cruise.

    C. Anything under a hundred bucks.

11. The phrase "not in your lifetime" refers to:

    A. Him cleaning the bathroom.

    B. Her cleaning out the gutters.

    C. Either of you ever cleaning the stuff that grows under the vegetable crisper in the refrigerator.

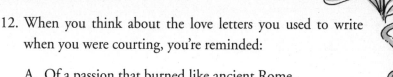

12. When you think about the love letters you used to write when you were courting, you're reminded:

    A. Of a passion that burned like ancient Rome.

    B. Of a love that will last for an eternity.

    C. That writing corny love letters is not a crime.

13. Often men and women will show subtle signs of stress and strain in different ways. For each way listed below, choose the most appropriate gender.

    A. Punch inanimate object, such as door or steering wheel.
       Male   Female   Either

    B. Make sniffling noises and sigh heavily.
       Male   Female   Either

    C. Blame clubs, bats, bowling balls, etc. for poor athletic performance.
       Male   Female   Either

    D. Clamp hands over face and weep. When questioned, keep saying, "Oh, nothing" over and over.
       Male   Female   Either

14. When the both of you attend church together, it is best for the husband to wear:

    A. A dark suit.

    B. A tuxedo.

    C. Whatever his wife picks out.

15. When the waiter asks what you'd like for dessert, a wife's most common response is:

    A. "Chocolate mousse, please."

    B. "I'll try the cheesecake."

    C. "Oh, nothing for me. I'll just have a teensie bite of his."

16. Your husband tries on his high school jacket and finds he can no longer snap it up. A wife's best response is:

    A. "Maybe it shrunk."

    B. "I like you a little less skinny."

    C. "That jacket would look dumb on a bald guy anyway."

17. Some household chores are traditionally done by the man, some by the woman. Place the following chores in the correct category:

    A. Cooking.
       Him   Her

    B. Flattening couch cushions.
       Him   Her

    C. Cleaning.
       Him   Her

    D. Tossing newspaper sections around.
       Him   Her

    E. Dusting.
       Him   Her

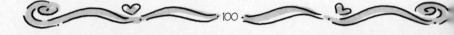

F. Snoring on Saturday afternoon.

Him   Her

18. Your spouse is snoring. You should:

A. Accept it as a minor flaw in an otherwise perfect mate.

B. Gently nudge him and say, "Roll over, dear."

C. Put a pair of sweatpants over his head and tighten the drawstring.

19. Who wants which addition to the house?

A. A cozy breakfast nook.

Wife   Husband

B. A red velour wallpapered den with big leather couches and a pinball machine and a pool table and a moosehead and a telephone that looks like a football helmet and a huge screen television set and a stereo with tapes of every college basketball game ever played and a train set and (well you get the idea)…

Wife   Husband

20. When riding with your husband on long car trips, you use the hours of quiet time to:

A. Discuss meaningful topics.

B. Point out the beauty of the scenery.

C. Excitedly warn him of impending highway danger that you can barely see as a tiny speck on the horizon.

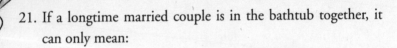

21. If a longtime married couple is in the bathtub together, it can only mean:

    A. They still feel passionately about each other.

    B. Their love life is spontaneous and exciting.

    C. He's grouting some loose tile while she tries to get rid of stubborn soap scum.

22. TRUE OR FALSE: The husband often lets his wife answer the telephone because it's usually for her anyway.

    FALSE: The husband often lets his wife answer the telephone because, if he doesn't, he may end up talking to her mother.

23. The phrase most often heard when the two of you are alone in a quiet setting is:

    A. "I love you."

    B. "I need you."

    C. "Zzzzzzzz…"

24. When doing the laundry, which of the following is the average husband most likely to forget?

    A. Whites in hot.

    B. Colors in cold.

    C. Pens, pencils, keys, tissues, etc. in pockets.

25. A husband offers to run to the store for a quart of milk. He is most likely to return with:

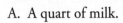

A. A quart of milk.

B. Two steaks, a big fish, a bottle of ketchup, two bottles of pop, a box of donuts, a TV dinner, some cheese, the latest issue of *TV Guide,* and a can of 40-weight motor oil.

C. A dazed expression and the question, "What was I supposed to get?"

26. (Husband question) To prove your love for your wife, you would gladly:

    A. Climb the highest mountain.

    B. Swim the deepest ocean.

    C. Hold her purse while she tries things on at the mall and run the risk that, at any moment, one of the guys might walk by.

27. (Wife question) To prove your love for your husband, you would gladly:

    A. Climb the highest mountain.

    B. Swim the deepest ocean.

    C. Put gas in the car at one of those self-serve places where the risk of a broken fingernail is a constant threat.

Would You Let Me Woo You?

Laura Jensen Walker

"Would you *let* me woo you?" my brand-new husband snapped at me on the fourth day of our marriage.

I looked up in surprise from the pile of wedding gifts I was sorting through. After all, we'd already spent a few blissful days at a charming bed-and-breakfast at the start of our week-long honeymoon. But now we were home in our tiny one-bedroom apartment, and I was eager to get settled and put everything in its place.

Michael was eager for the honeymoon to continue.

After all, he was a newlywed with just two more days left of his vacation before he had to return to work and the "real world."

Me too.

Except that I didn't want the work week to start with my new home in disarray. To me—the formerly dyed-in-the-wool

romantic—it was important to get organized so that we'd return to an orderly home where we could relax at the end of a hard day. I couldn't relax in a room full of wrapping paper and discarded boxes.

Michael didn't understand. During our dating days, I couldn't get enough romance. Now here I was on our honeymoon preferring cleaning to an impromptu picnic he'd planned!

That was the first inkling he had that he'd dated Jekyll, married Hyde.

Camping was next.

While we were dating, I'd regaled Michael with stories of rafting excursions, hikes, and camping trips from the days when I was in the singles leadership group at church. This led him to believe that I was at least a tiny bit out-

That was the first inkling he had that he'd dated Jekyll, married Hyde.

doorsy. But what I had neglected to tell him was my motive behind all those outdoor excursions: a man.

I'd had a crush on one guy for years who never saw me as anything more than a friend and sister in Christ. But I was so besotted with this hiking and backpacking man that I did anything I could just to be near him. Even camp.

So poor Michael thinks he's marrying this exciting, adventurous woman who will hike and camp and spend countless hours in the great outdoors with him.

What he didn't know is that I am a slug.

Not that I have anything against spending time outside. In fact, there's nothing quite like the wind in my hair as I'm reading. Or the sound of chirping birds mingling with the sound of turning pages.

Whereas Michael had something a little more active in mind.

Our first camping trip took place two months after we were married. We went to the ocean with a large mixed group of singles and couples. Realizing by now that camping wasn't high on my list of fun things to do, Michael did everything he could to make it a pleasant experience. Starting with the monster tent he bought.

Everyone else had either a one-man pup tent or one of those two-person dome-style jobbies. Ours was a condominium in comparison. Large and luxurious, Michael thought that even I could be happy in a tent like this.

> I didn't find it particularly romantic when I woke up freezing the next morning with sand embedded in my skin.

I helped him set up our deluxe outdoor accommodations, then went to visit with some friends around the campfire. Half an hour later, Michael joined us. But after just a few minutes of polite conversation, he nudged me and said it was getting late.

He ushered me up the hill to our condo tent and unzipped the entrance with a flourish. Inside, the lantern, although turned down low, cast just enough light to illuminate the double-wide sleeping bag invitingly turned down atop the pumped-up air mattress.

To Michael, sleeping in a tent in the great outdoors was a romantic haven. However, I didn't find it particularly romantic when I woke up freezing the next morning with sand embedded in my skin and desperately needing to go to the bathroom—a mere half mile away.

As far as I was concerned, I didn't care if I ever saw the inside

of a tent again. But because I'm a supportive, loving wife who wants to make her husband happy by camping one weekend a year—when the temperature is just right, not too cold and not too hot—we load up the car and head to one of California's beautiful campgrounds. (I just make sure to pack plenty of insect repellent, extra socks, and a bagful of books.)

Michael's not the only one who dated Jekyll, married Hyde.

One of my girlfriends said that when she and her husband were dating, they snuggled on the couch to watch a football game together. He thought it was because she enjoyed the game.

Not exactly.

"It was because I wanted to snuggle, not because I wanted to watch football," she said. Since they've been married, she hasn't watched one game. She doesn't need to. Now she's found other avenues of snuggling.

Then there's another friend whose husband, an avid skier, had visions of them schussing down the slopes together. She likes to ski, she's just not in the same class as he is. So he decided to help out by giving her the benefit of his expertise.

She decided she'd rather learn from a professional instructor.

Only problem was the instructor was a cute, perky "snow-bunny" who paid more attention to her husband than to her.

So much for skiing.

Still another friend said that while they were dating, her husband always ran his car through a car wash before picking her up for a date. "It was always immaculate, and I was really impressed," she told me.

Since they've been wed, the car has not seen the inside of a car wash.

We all have areas of great expectations in our marriage.

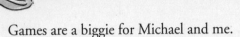

Games are a biggie for Michael and me.

During our courtship, we got together often with friends for many fun-filled, fiercely competitive evenings playing board games. Yet another one of the many things my darling and I have in common.

Except that Michael expected the games to continue once we were married—with just the two of us.

Boring with a capital B. It's just not as much fun to pursue trivia *a deux*.

But then came the evening when we discovered strip *Monopoly*.

Time to Go: Ready or Not

Laura Jensen Walker

Men and women tell time differently.

Ask any husband.

For instance, a couple plans to go somewhere, and he'll say, "I'm ready." He grabs the keys and heads for the door.

But she's not ready.

She's just ready to *start* getting ready. Ten minutes later she's still in the bathroom.

Meanwhile, getting antsy, her husband leaves his post at the front door to tinker with something.

When she finally emerges from putting the finishing touches on her hair and makeup, she notices her husband busy doing something, so decides to just "straighten up a bit" while she waits for him.

I speak from firsthand experience.

I admit I'm not the best judge of time, but given that numbers are involved, you'd think Michael would be a little more understanding since he knows I'm math-challenged.

The reality is, I'm just trying to be considerate of my husband.

After all, once I've finished getting ready and notice that he's out puttering in the garden or working in the garage, I naturally don't want to interrupt—that would be rude.

Instead, I find something to do to occupy myself until *he's* ready.

Meanwhile, he's outside being productive, thinking he's waiting for me.

When he finally finishes whatever it is he's doing and comes inside to see me straightening up the kitchen, he gets frustrated and says, "C'mon, honey. We're going to be late!"

"I'm ready," I'll say innocently. "I'm just waiting for you."

I don't understand why this bugs him so much.

"Jill" can relate.

"I'm dressed, ready to go, so my husband gets ready," she says.

"He's ready, opening the door thinking I'm right behind him—because I'm 'ready,' right?—and I'm elsewhere to be found—putting dishes away, cleaning up the kitchen, applying last-minute touches to my makeup.

"*Now* when I say I'm ready, my husband doesn't move from his chair, knowing full well that it's just a five-minute warning till I'm really ready."

Her husband has figured out that she's really and truly ready once she's standing at the door saying, "Ready to go?"

It's flip-flopped in our marriage.

Our problem begins in the shower.

I take a five-minute shower and need about twenty minutes afterward to get ready, while Michael takes twenty-minute showers and only needs five minutes to get ready.

Therefore, Michael logically thinks that if I shower first, then I have twenty minutes to get ready while he's showering.

And once he gets out and dresses, we'll both be ready to go.

It doesn't work that way.

That's because I'm in my own time zone.

While he's showering, I spend those twenty minutes doing other things around the house—checking my e-mail, unloading the dishwasher, etc.

Once I hear the shower stop, I know that I now have twenty minutes to get ready.

Naturally, Michael always finishes getting ready before me, and has to wait.

Once I'm finished and on my way to the door, I can't find Michael, so I call out impatiently, "C'mon, honey, we've got to get going or we'll be late!"

Good thing those marriage vows say "for better or for worse."

One way I've found to beat my time gauge problem is to set every clock in the house to a different time.

Our bedroom alarm clock is half an hour fast—at Michael's insistence, so he has the perceived luxury of sleeping in—the clock on the VCR in the den is five minutes slow (which I keep meaning to change since I always miss the beginning of *Jeopardy*), and the clock in my office is ten minutes fast so I can feel I've accomplished a lot in a short period of time.

The only problem is, I sometimes confuse the VCR clock with my office clock and wind up late anyway.

This time problem isn't peculiar only to married couples either.

For instance, Jared Frederick Budenski, a psychology major at Dakota Wesleyan University, sent me an e-mail about one date he'll never forget.

"This girl and I were planning to go out for a soda and just to hang out, then we were going to go for a walk and watch a video," Jared said. "When I called her to see if she was ready to go, she said come on up."

The problem was, Jared lived only two minutes away from his date, and when he arrived to pick her up, she wasn't quite ready. So her parents intercepted and he spent an awkward fifteen minutes—or an eternity—making small talk with them.

"Finally, she came out ready to go," Jared said. "She had her hair done, perfume on, the whole nine yards, and I just had on a T-shirt and pants."

The two went out for soda and hung out awhile just having fun, then decided to go on their walk. The only problem was, before his date could take a walk, she said she needed to change into athletic clothes.

Which took another fifteen minutes. (More small talk with the folks.)

But Jared says the walk was nice and they had a good conversation, then came back to watch the video.

However, before sitting down in front of the TV, his date said she needed to change, so she took a shower and changed out of her athletic clothes into a nice outfit—which took another thirty minutes.

By that time, Jared said, he could almost have watched the video.

"I guess 'I'm ready' really meant 'give me an extra hour,'" he said. Just wait till he gets married.

a houseful of laughs

Presidential Candidates
—MARGARET THATCHER,
IN THE OBSERVER, MAY 8, 1979

Any woman who understands the problems of running a home will be nearer to understanding the problems of running a country.

Dare to Decorate

Lynn Bowen Walker

To be honest, the whole idea of redecorating unnerves me.

My husband and I are an unlikely decorating match to begin with. I brought color to our union: bright orange and neon green, to be exact, a color combination I can explain only by saying I was the last girl scout to choose my fabric on patchwork pillow-making day, and it seemed to me after investing so much time in hand sewing, I was committed.

Mark brought to our marriage the sophisticated taste and affluence of your typical college man: a basketball hoop laundry hamper, slatted wooden crates that grocery stores use to sell lugs of fruit and a collection of dark wooden objects decoupaged with American eagles that I can classify only as "paperweights."

A family therapist might see the merging of our two childhood bedroom sets as an abstract metaphor for the oneness of marriage.

Whatever.

All I know is that for the past 17 years our entire decorating strategy has revolved around ditching the most offensive of the cast-offs that served as our dowries, including the orange fish net that once draped artfully across the living room wall and the brown canvas rocker that swallowed fannies the way the Venus flytrap sucks up flies.

Somehow the massive, mud-colored, faux-wood dressers in our bedroom have managed to escape being overthrown. For some reason (I remember now, money) they've remained, flanking our bed like sentries.

But their days are numbered. The deal was clinched after a recent visit from some over-zealous children who like to jump. We looked at our cockeyed bed frame and realized it had hosted its last Pee-Wee Olympics. While we were at it, it seemed we might as well junk the clunky dressers too and buy something that didn't scream to be accessorized with black velvet Elvis paintings.

Since it's taken all these years simply to arrive at an uninspired, nondescript middle ground we could both live with, I was not approaching redecorating with high hopes. It would be lovely to find a style that made both our hearts sing, but in the back of my mind I feared being overpowered by both my husband and some flashy style-monger salesman who'd be pushing gold brocade Louis XIV settees.

Plus it was hard to shake the nagging question: is decorating really practical, anyway? I have yet to see in the glossy decorating books even a hint of dirty laundry. And where do the owners of those rooms keep the 40-pound bag of dog food? Should you just color-coordinate the bag to match the linoleum? Better yet, just color-coordinate the dog? "I'd like a taupe dog, please, to match the great room. Low-pile, preferably," you could say brightly.

These were valid questions. But can you really debate a broken bed? Circumstances seemed to dictate that it was time to redecorate (or more to the point, to decorate in the first place). Not trusting our own instincts (after all, we've lived with this stuff for 17 years; surely any sense of good taste we once had is blunted), we trooped to the furniture store to snag a decorator to help us.

As it turns out, my worries were unfounded. The decorator came last week. She was great.

"We're pretty casual," I said in what is perhaps the understatement of the year, guiding her back to our bedroom past little league cleats on the piano and dog-ingested tennis ball bits. Our dressers, which were last cleared off in 1989, sported mounds of papers and dog-eared magazines.

But this lady had mastered Decorator Tact 101. Seeing the paper debris, she had a ready answer. "You must be readers," she offered. Ecstatic at

> Our entire decorating strategy has revolved around ditching the most offensive of the cast-offs.

her insight into our finer qualities, I was ready to buy whatever she was selling.

Working us like a Vegas crowd, she continued, "My nightstands at home look just like yours." I eyed her color-coordinated eye makeup, earrings and scarf and had a hard time picturing her bedroom strewn with half-finished super-hero artwork and peanut butter toast crusts. But I simply nodded and pretended to believe her.

"Could we move the bucket?" she suggested gently, pointing to the pail in the corner we use to catch rainwater.

"We'll be re-roofing soon," we assured her.

Tossing off terms like focal point, balance and scale, she waxed eloquent about the finer points of our room—among them, the open beam down the middle of the ceiling. I felt bad that I'd never appreciated these features as assets.

I simply nodded and pretended to believe her.

As we discussed hitherto unfamiliar furniture styles, I tried to picture each "piece" as it would actually look in our home: covered with Legos.

We finally made our decisions (cherry wood in a Country French style and already "distressed" to save us the trouble). The decorator graciously left, leaving us to bask in the glow of the thought of furniture that will arrive on our doorstep as its very first stop.

We'd done it. We'd survived redecorating, marriage and egos intact. That left us with just one last hurdle to jump.

Happen to know any newlyweds who'd like some dressers? Tell 'em if they don't look too closely, they almost look like real wood.

When You Can't Take It with You

Martha Bolton

Have you ever wondered what you'd take if you suddenly had to be evacuated? Now, granted, if you only had five minutes, you'd grab the kids and the pets, and quickly be on your way to safety.

But what if you had a half-hour notice? Or an hour? Or even a half-day? You know, just enough time to be selective. Have you considered what things you'd most want to save? What items around your house do you feel are irreplaceable?

Not long ago, my husband and I tried making our list.

"The antiques should be first on the list," he began.

"Why?" I asked. "My dresses can always be replaced."

He continued, undaunted.

"And our most important papers should be next."

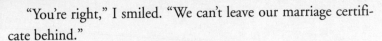

"You're right," I smiled. "We can't leave our marriage certificate behind."

"Marriage certificate? I was talking about my *Golf Digest* subscription receipt."

"Well, what about my pictures of Mom?" I inquired.

"This is an emergency. We won't have time to rent a U-haul."

"I'm definitely not leaving my awards behind," I said, emphatically.

"No, we'll take those," he conceded. "But I'm warning you, between them and your fan mail, we won't be able to fit anything else into the glove compartment of the car."

Ignoring that comment, I continued.

"I'm taking my typewriter."

"I'm taking my fishing poles and tackle box," he countered.

"I'm taking my scrapbooks."

"I'm taking my bowling ball."

"I'm taking my collector's plates."

"I'm taking the VCR."

This continued until, at least on paper, we had our entire house loaded into and on top of our car.

"We may have to leave some things behind," I said, realizing if we were to evacuate, ideally we should make it out of the driveway.

We both looked over the list once more.

"OK," we said, finally agreeing on something. "The bill box can stay."

No wonder the Bible tells us to lay up our treasures in heaven.

Handy Dandy
Rooster Repairs
Fran Caffey Sandin

One day while shopping for my household items, I spied a padded potty seat. Remembering our ancient bathroom with the cracked and peeling lid, I thought…*hey, we need one of those.* So after propitiously pondering the proper decision, I purchased the pink one with embroidered flowers on the lid and hurried home.

Eager to see my new "touch of class" in place, I carried it in from the car, grabbed a small wrench, and skipped toward our bathroom to detach the old lid.

Kneeling beside the commode, I tried to unscrew the metal bolts. The left screw rotated 'round and 'round, but the bolt never loosened. Then I sat on the floor straddling the bowl, awkwardly hugging it as I reached around, straining to unscrew the left and then the right. Nothing happened. My farm-girl experiences had prepared me to tackle all kinds of fix-it problems from

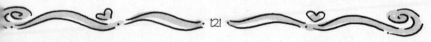

vacuum cleaner repairs to assembling furniture. But the hefty potty seat would not budge, so I asked my husband, Jim, to flex his muscles and give me a hand. After all, my urologist hubby was sort of a plumber anyway.

"Show me the new potty seat and I'll be glad to put it on," Jim agreed brightly, flashing his confident Superman smile. Sensing that "he-men" need room to work, I stepped into the next room to fold clothes.

At first I heard nothing but a little scooting about and Jim's cheerful whistling. A minute or two later, however, his whistling was punctuated by a few groans and "ughs." Then Jim darted to the garage for a screwdriver. After more clanking and grunting, he headed for the garage again and reappeared with a larger tool. His face was as red as a rooster's comb, and I was beginning to worry.

> His face was as red as a rooster's comb, and I was beginning to worry.

"Are you having a little trouble, dear?" I asked sheepishly.

"Oh, you know how these old metal bolts are—both are frozen in place."

Soon he began beating metal against metal to loosen the bolts before trying again to unscrew them. Jim struggled and tugged about half an hour before announcing, "I'm taking a break."

While he rested in the den, I had an idea. Perhaps he had loosened the bolts enough that I could waltz in, unscrew the old, put on the new, and surprise him. Surveying the situation, I noticed that dirt particles had fallen into the water. Without thinking, I reached up to flush the commode. As soon as my hand left

the handle, I knew I'd made a terrible mistake. A geyser the size of "Old Faithful" spurted out the side of the bowl. "Jim, help!" I yelled, jumping back away from the spray.

"Hey, what are you doing? What happened? Let me through so I can turn off the water," Jim shouted, rushing by me and reaching below the stool for the turn-off valve. Then I saw the panicked look in his eyes as it dawned on him that our old plumbing did not include one.

The water level continued to rise as Jim raced to the garage to find the long-handled rod for cutting off the water main in front of the house. Then he had to dig a hole in the flower bed to get to it. In the meantime, I pulled the towels off the racks and used them as sandbags to keep the water from flooding the adjoining bedrooms. Then I attempted to scoop up some of the water and pour it into the shower stall with a small cleaning bucket I found under the sink.

The only nice thing about that Saturday was the bright sunshine outside. Everything went downhill fast. Once the water had been turned off, we examined the wreckage and discovered that the porcelain stool was cracked. We had no choice but to replace the entire fixture. Oh, the joys of home ownership!

Jim, normally a happy guy, took on the demeanor of a bulldog while I searched the bookshelf for *Will This Marriage Survive?* After numerous growls and three more trips to the hardware store, Jim, with steam emanating from his ears, successfully installed a new commode, a turn-off valve, a main cut-off valve, and my new potty seat. (By the way, it's lovely.)

Realizing that my husband had spent his entire day off on this simple project, I apologized for the trouble I'd caused, crowned

him "My Hero," and baked a batch of his favorite Deer Valley Cowboy Cookies.

Last Christmas, we had a kind of encore. A few minutes before our company was to arrive, I decided to tidy up the utility bathroom. When I flushed the commode, it kept running, running, and running. Then water began spilling over the top. I frantically jiggled the handle to no avail, and then, lifted the tank lid. Imagine my astonishment as a powerful stream of water hit the ceiling and showered back down on my head. Reaching inside the tank, I located the broken metal part and held my hand over it to stop the flow. I felt about as desperate as the Dutch boy with his finger in the dike.

That's when I spotted a turn-off valve near the baseboard. So I stuffed a towel in the tank and tried with all my strength to turn the valve. It seemed welded into place. Plunging in another towel as reinforcement, I raced to the garage for the pipe wrench and applied that to the stubborn valve, but despite my twists and turns, it would not budge.

Jim was running errands in town so I beeped him. When he called from his car phone, I cried, "Jim, our commode in the utility room just blew up. Water is flying everywhere and I can't fix it!" Knowing what he would ask, I added, "I can't turn off the valve."

"I'm on my way home," he said calmly, "but in the meantime, call the plumber."

So at 4:00 P.M. on December 23, I phoned a local plumber, who said that if I would go and buy a new commode, he would come by and install it. "I'm in a hurry," he stressed. "Go shopping right away."

A few minutes later, our daughter, son-in-law, and grand-daughter drove in the back driveway and entered through the open back door. When they walked around the corner, they stopped short. There I was (peering through my new string-mop hairdo, mascara dripping down my face) standing over the commode with both hands in the tank, trying to control Niagara Falls. I briefly explained the situation to them as Jim arrived. We placed a brick over the leak, turned off the main water valve, and hurried off to the store.

He and I were laughing as we drove to the lumberyard just before closing time to buy another Christmas present for each other. Jim was in such a jovial mood, I asked him to make the selection. He decided in thirty seconds, and without debate, I said, "We'll take it."

I felt about as desperate as the Dutch boy with his finger in the dike.

After the plumbers, Billy and Dale, had removed the old fixture and replaced it with the new, Billy stood back and gazed at his handiwork. "You know Dale, that toilet for the handicapped looks real nice in here. I think I'll get me one of them."

Jim and I looked at each other and gasped. "A potty for the handicapped?"

"Oh, yes Ma'am," he said. "This is one of those *real high* ones."

"My six-foot, four-inch husband thinks it's perfect," I said, smiling, "but the rest of us may need a ladder." I quickly placed greenery and a big red bow on top for decoration and thanked the plumbers from rescuing us from the flood.

Looking back, I can better see the value of situations like these. Through them, Jim and I learned to be more flexible and not take everything so seriously, including our plumbing problems. After all, life is full of unpredictable events. We've also learned a few other things—like the value of kindness, and most of all, the unmeasurable worth of a good sense of humor.

bringing up
laughter
—more parenting humor

Raising Kids
—Ed Asner

Raising kids is part joy and part guerilla warfare.

Private: No Trespassing

Karen Scalf Linamen

It's nice to be sought after. But sometimes you can get too much of a good thing. My pet peeve is hearing a knock on the bathroom door followed by the familiar words, "What are you doing in there?"

What do they think I'm doing?

Maybe kids have this weird fear that, while *their* bathroom time is reserved for boring functions of elimination, grownups aren't bound by the same rules. Maybe they think we hide out in the bathroom so we can do really cool things we don't let *them* do, like eating Gummi Bears before dinner and watching cartoons when our homework isn't done. That's why we lock the door. We don't want our children to know we're having all the fun.

Not only is bathroom time not sacred but personal space is up for grabs as well. Literally.

I knew a woman who once dressed her seven-year-old daughter as a "Mommy" for Halloween. She put curlers in her daughter's hair, smeared jelly on her shirt, and tied an apron around her waist. But the *pièce de résistance* was the baby doll strapped to her leg.

We all know what that feels like, don't we?

I don't know about your experience with little ones, but my babies didn't believe in pacifiers and security blankets. After all, why should they cling to a threadbare piece of cloth when they could cling to me? Kaitlyn's comfort item of choice was my earlobe. She hung on when she was bored, scared, or tired. She considered my earrings a very personal affront.

> By the time we're mothers, we don't have any private parts left.

Kacie got a little more personal than that. She's three and she still thinks my right armpit belongs to her. That and my mole. It's on my left shoulder blade. One day she skinned her knee on the driveway. After I patched her up she was still crying. I offered hugs, popsicles, gum, and more. She wouldn't stop crying. Finally, through her tears, she said, "I want your mole." She wrapped her arms around my neck, slipped a hand under my shirt, found my mole, hiccupped once, and stopped crying.

I teach my kids the concept of personal space, and the idea that there are parts of their body that are private. For my daughters, I've described these areas as parts of the body that would be covered up by a two-piece bathing suit. What I don't tell them is that this definition will apply until they become mothers. Somehow, in the process of conceiving a baby, birthing a baby,

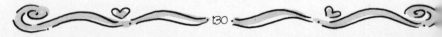

and nursing a baby, everything's up for grabs. Between husbands, nurses, doctors, and our newborns, every "private part" we ever had seems to become public property.

I remember when I was giving birth to Kaitlyn. I had just passed my pain threshold and asked—no, begged—for some drugs. In no time at all the Demerol took effect and ushered me into la-la-land. I know I was in la-la-land because I remember looking at my husband and saying thickly, "Honey, could you close the kitchen door? I think I feel a breeze."

Was I in the kitchen? Of course not. That was the Demerol talking. Did I feel a breeze? What do you think? The way the LDR door kept revolving with hospital staff, gusts in that room must have been approaching 20 mph—and me wearing nothing but a paper gown and metal stirrups. No doubt windchill was a factor. It's a miracle I didn't have to be treated for frostbite at some point after crowning and before my episiotomy. Breeze? That's an understatement: I was experiencing high winds in my area of my anatomy where the sun never shines.

Privacy. Hah!

By the time we're mothers, we don't have any private parts left. The skimpiest bathing suit wouldn't reveal anything we haven't already revealed to total strangers in lab coats.

And what about privacy when it comes to our personal belongings? We spend years trying to teach our children the nuances of sharing. We talk about greed versus generosity, selfishness versus selfless giving. We model and lecture and teach and inspire. And after we have expended all our words on the subject, what our children manage to conclude from our vast outpouring of wisdom and insights in that what's ours is theirs and what's theirs is theirs, too.

The family car? Theirs. The balance in the checkbook? Theirs. Mom's favorite cashmere sweater and Dad's secret stash of Wintergreen Lifesavers? Theirs, theirs, theirs.

My children have already informed me which pieces of my jewelry they want when I die.

I remember once, when Kaitlyn was about four, feeling tired after a long day filled with Barbies and Big Bird. I felt like I needed a break from my role as Social Director and Principal Plaything for our daughter. She was begging me to play hide-and-seek when I spoke up in frustration: "Kaitlyn, we've been playing for hours! What do you think I am, a toy?"

Kaitlyn looked at me, and without batting an eyelash, said, "Yes."

Well. That explains a lot, doesn't it?

After all, toys are on call twenty-four hours a day. They have no personal space and get no respect. They don't have any possessions. Half the time they don't even get to wear clothes.

But maybe I should count my blessings. I might not get any more privacy than Barbie, but at least my elbows bend.

The Outlaws of Physics
Renae Bottom

Einstein was wrong.

Einstein, Newton and all the brilliant thinkers who gave us physics as we know it shared a common law: They based their postulations solely on their study of the larger universe. That's the big place outside your front door where things run on time and the only forces to be reckoned with are nice, orderly ones like gravity and the motion of planets.

These men didn't know about kids.

They didn't know the mere fact of a child's presence immediately alters all known formulas for predicting the behavior of objects in the physical world.

Take, for instance, the famous law of physics Angle of Incidence Equals Angle of Reflection. I think this means if a

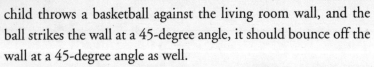
child throws a basketball against the living room wall, and the ball strikes the wall at a 45-degree angle, it should bounce off the wall at a 45-degree angle as well.

Now, any parent knows this isn't true. If a child throws a basketball against the living room wall, it will bounce off the wall and knock over a lamp (antique), a potted plant (exotic), and some smaller child (probably a fussy neighbor's), regardless of the wild and illogical angles required to accomplish it.

It happens because the Basketball Thrown in the House Must Knock Over Three Items Before It Comes to Rest law far outweighs anything Newton ever came up with.

> The potential energy of any object increases exponentially with the object's value.

And remember those other great concepts, "potential" and "kinetic" energy? Physics tells us an object raised off the ground acquires potential energy. If the object falls, this potential energy is expressed as motion, or kinetic energy.

Beautiful logic, but someone forgot to factor in a few pertinent intangibles. Like, in a household with children, the potential energy of any object increases exponentially with the object's value. And if the object is both expensive and filled with something sure to stain the carpet? You'd better call NASA to handle the numbers. For example: With a child present, a $100 crystal carafe brimming with grape juice and perched on the dining-room table (over the cashmere rug) possesses potential energy roughly equivalent to that of Disney's Big Red Boat perched atop EPCOT Center.

And the kinetic energy achieved by this carafe after a 2-year-old enters the room?

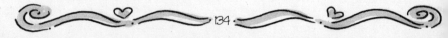

Don't even ask. Just phone the carpet service and have your credit card handy.

Other laws of physics, observed daily by parents but unexplained by textbooks:

- Toast flung from a highchair always lands jelly-side down.

- Water draining from a child's bath generates the precise force required to propel action figures halfway down the drain.

- A child who trips never falls down until he achieves the specific direction and momentum necessary to bring his head in contact with the nearest piece of unpadded furniture.

- A baby's fingers, when wrapped around human hair, can exert pressures of up to 9,000 pounds per square inch.

- And that Theory of Relativity you've heard so much about? It has nothing to do with the proposed effects of travel at light speed. It really means when your children do something horrendous, they're behaving just like your spouse's relatives. When they do something tremendously clever, it's obvious they take after your side of the family.

If theoretical physicists with children weren't so busy replacing broken windows and smoothing it over with Grandma about the heirloom china, they might have time to publish such facts. As it is, our physics texts are likely to remain as they are, reliable as they relate to the motion of atomic particles, but wholly inaccurate as they predict the havoc wrought by children.

So much in science remains to be done.

A Hiding Place

Martha Bolton

Why is it on those mornings when you oversleep and have 15 minutes to get the kids to school, nothing seems to go right?

I recall one morning in particular when this happened. I found myself racing to my sons' bedrooms. Pausing briefly in each doorway, I tenderly smiled upon their sleepy innocence, then lovingly yanked off the covers and whispered, "GET UP AND GET OUT OF BED! YOU'RE LATE FOR SCHOOL!"

Trusting them to dress themselves, I hurried to the kitchen to burn, I mean, cook breakfast. After five minutes and two more announcements, though, I still didn't hear the sounds of busy little feet scurrying to get dressed.

"You'd better be out of bed," I warned as I returned to check on their progress.

They were out of bed all right but had fallen back to sleep in the shirt drawer.

"You have exactly two minutes to dress and eat," I ordered, "I'll be waiting for you in the car."

"You're not taking us to school like that, are you?" questioned my eldest son, Rusty.

"No one will see me," I assured him, repinning a curler.

"But there's green crud on your face."

"It's not crud. It's an herbal mask, and I don't have time to take it off. Now hurry!"

Grabbing the keys off the table, I went outside to start warming the car's engine.

Moments later, my middle son, Matt, a first grader at the time, appeared in the doorway.

"The Superman cape goes," I said, snatching it from his shoulders as he hopped into the car.

Rusty followed next and passed inspection.

Then, Tony, the youngest, appeared, but for some reason looked taller than usual.

"Why are you wearing skates?" I inquired, glancing down at his feet.

"I can't find my shoes," he shrugged.

Biting my lip, I turned off the motor and ran back inside the house to look for his shoes, or for that matter, any shoes without wheels; but the only matching pair I could find were bronzed. While I contemplated cramming his feet into those, Matt honked the car horn, signaling he had found Tony's shoes under the front seat of the car.

At last, we were ready to go, and it was a race against the

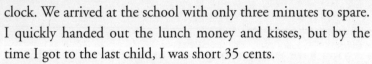
clock. We arrived at the school with only three minutes to spare. I quickly handed out the lunch money and kisses, but by the time I got to the last child, I was short 35 cents.

Emptying my purse onto my lap turned up seven more pennies and the Sears catalog I had been looking for. A quick check in the ashtray netted another nickel and four rusted bobby pins. Hauling the carseats out onto the curb uncovered three more cents and a video game token.

"Why don't we just borrow the money from the principal?" Rusty suggested. "He's coming this way."

I quickly hid under the dashboard, hoping he'd think the boys drove themselves to school. But it didn't work. He knew I was there and wanted to know why my carseats were blocking the school bus. I explained I was looking for lunch money. He graciously gave me the change I needed, then helped me put the seats back in the car.

Thanking him for his kindness, I sent the boys off to their classes and pulled away. All I wanted to do was go home. The sooner, the better. But I only made it as far as the corner before running out of gas.

As I sat there stalled in the middle of the street, I wanted to cry, but the green crud on my face wouldn't give.

It was starting to rain now, and there was only one thing I could do. I had to gather up what little dignity I had left and start walking toward the nearest gas station.

But then again you can only look just so dignified hauling a gas can down the main street of town in curlers and Mickey Mouse pajamas with the feet in them.

At times like this, isn't it nice to know we can hide in His love?

humor
with a
shine

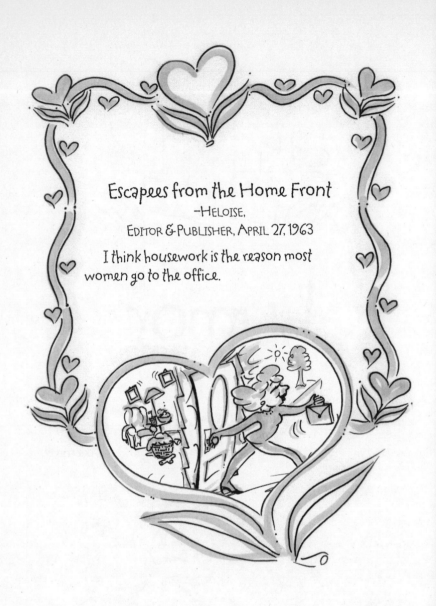

Escapees from the Home Front
—HELOISE,
EDITOR & PUBLISHER, APRIL 27, 1963

I think housework is the reason most women go to the office.

Mapping Out Mom's Cleaning Strategy

Marti Attoun

Spring cleaning is a pillow-fluff compared with that deadly summer ritual of cleaning for long-distance relatives.

This requires some math, along with a mop. The depth of cleaning is directly proportional to the distance these folks travel. You won't find this cleaning formula among Heloise's hints, but it's been understood and passed down from one generation of dusters to the next. (The formula is diluted, however, with each passing.)

For example, my mother switches into high cleaning gear several weeks before a visit from an out-of-stater. She's been known to paint rooms, hose down the house siding, and mop the driveway to prepare for a visit from her sister, who lives 2,000 miles away.

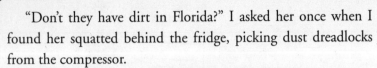

"Don't they have dirt in Florida?" I asked her once when I found her squatted behind the fridge, picking dust dreadlocks from the compressor.

"Not as much as we do in the Midwest. You know your Aunt Geraldine is clean as a pin," she informed me. "Here, I'm going to tip the fridge while you sweep off the *bottom*."

This same guest triggers an all-nighter of aerobic cleaning at my place, which basically involves herding the dust motes from the house into the garage. This is followed by a threat—to the kids and the motes: "Don't you dare open the garage door until the coast is clear."

After years of observation, I've calculated Mom's cleaning formula. For a visit from a relative or friend who lives within 25 miles, she wipes down the dining-room table. For 25 to 100 miles, she adds a vinyl tablecloth. For 100 to 1,000 miles, she starches and irons the embroidered peacock tablecloth.

For the 1,000-miles-and-more crowd, she refinishes the table.

The 25-miles-and-under folks rate a new roll of toilet paper. The 1,000-milers get the show soaps, arranged like pastel candy mints in the heart-shaped soap dish.

The short-distance guests get fried bologna sandwiches on paper plates. The long-distance guys get roast beef and homemade cobbler on matching china (atop the embroidered peacock, of course).

I admire my mother's cleaning formula, but it definitely shows signs of fading through the generations. You won't find any moth carcasses in her light fixtures. You won't find any light bulbs in mine.

Chronic Purse-Stuffers Club

Renae Bottom

How much does your purse weigh? Five pounds? Ten? Fifteen? If you've decided not to purchase free weights for your home because carrying your purse provides all the strength training you need, welcome to the Chronic Purse-Stuffers Club. Anyone can join. Those of us who already belong know who we are.

We're the ones whose shoulders are three inches lower on one side. We have savings accounts designated for rotator cuff surgery.

We've ceased worrying about that old advice from our mothers. You know, to wear clean underwear in case we're ever in an accident? We only worry that while we're unconscious, some poor soul will attempt to identify us by the contents of our purses. Horrifying.

Still, for all the teasing we take, those of us who belong to the Chronic Purse-Stuffers Club are handy to have around in an

emergency. Not only do we carry Kleenex, hairspray, cotton balls, plastic bandages, antacid tablets, and up to $100 in loose change, we also come equipped with a flare gun, a set of hand tools, a personal flotation device, and all the utensils necessary for preparing fresh game over an open fire.

I'm fairly certain I could defuse a bomb, using nothing but the contents of my purse. I'm positive I could make radio contact with the Pentagon. And I could probably set a broken leg and suture a small flesh wound. It's all part of who I am, a purse-toting pack rat.

If asked to admit this minor personality quirk, would I own up to it? Of course not, and neither should any other compulsive purse-stuffer. There's a perfectly logical explanation for all this stuff we carry around.

Like those old department store receipts, dating back to 1983? Those are kindling if I'm ever stranded in a blizzard and have to build a fire on short notice. And I could spread ketchup from my foil packets onto the cello-wrapped soda crackers I've been collecting from restaurant salad bars and have quite a tasty dinner if help didn't arrive until morning.

Then I could freshen up with a few moist towelettes from the fast-food drive through and wait for the rescue plane to arrive. It would soon spot my SOS message, outlined in the snow with bright red grocery discount stamps.

So you see, Chronic Purse-Stuffers are not unorganized. Just hyper-prepared, that's all. Don't any of you neat freaks tell me to clean out my purse—you never know when you might get hit by a bus and require first aid.

And besides, you wouldn't be foolish enough to provoke someone carrying a purse this heavy, would you?

It's Time to Clean Out the Fridge When...

Karen Scalf Linamen

Ever feel like whining?

I just got home from the supermarket. If anything makes me want to pull up a chair and whine, it's looking in the refrigerator and realizing I'm going to have to spend the next forty minutes getting intimate with last month's leftovers if I'm going to have a shot at getting this week's milk and eggs in cold storage.

I always know when it's time to clean out my refrigerator. It's time to clean out the fridge when I run out of Tupperware. I remember one time I cleaned out my refrigerator and ended up with so much Tupperware I got the hostess gift *plus* the stacking sandwich caddies.

Of course, one of the downsides of keeping leftovers around too long is that, at some point (and you're never quite sure exactly when this point occurs), the edible becomes inedible. I get

very stressed if I have to leave town on business for a couple of days, because I can't be certain my family fully understands the need to use discretion while looking for a quick meal. I know this is hard to believe, but they actually think they can just open the refrigerator door at any given moment and choose, willy-nilly, from among the options. They don't understand that choosing a leftover from the refrigerator at our house is a little like playing Russian Roulette. That's why I always look tired if I am flying out of town for a speaking engagement or book tour. It's not because my flight left at 7:00 A.M. It's because I stayed up until 3:00 A.M. cleaning out the refrigerator so no one dies of food poisoning while I'm away.

> Choosing a leftover from the refrigerator at our house is a little like playing Russian Roulette.

So far there have been no actual casualties. There are no notches on my refrigerator door. Close calls, however, are another story.

One morning I slept in. I was dead tired, having spent half the night nursing a two-year-old with a stuffy nose. As a result, my husband woke our eleven-year-old and helped her get ready for school. Since the school cafeteria was closed that week, he even made a sack lunch for her.

About ten that morning, Kacie and I sat down to breakfast. And suddenly I had a horrible thought.

I rushed to the phone and dialed Kaitlyn's school. I asked the puzzled secretary to pull Kaitlyn out of class and bring her to the phone. I told her it was an emergency.

"Mom?" Kaitlyn asked a moment later. "Everything okay?"

"Sweetie, Dad made your lunch this morning, right?"

"Right."

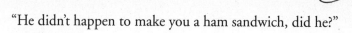

"He didn't happen to make you a ham sandwich, did he?"

"Yeah, he did."

"Don't eat it."

"Don't eat it?"

"Not unless you happen to have a stomach pump on hand. What time does your class break for lunch?"

"11:30."

"I'll be there."

I swung through McDonald's for a Happy Meal. That afternoon I threw out the ham.

12

how quickly they grow, how swiftly we laugh

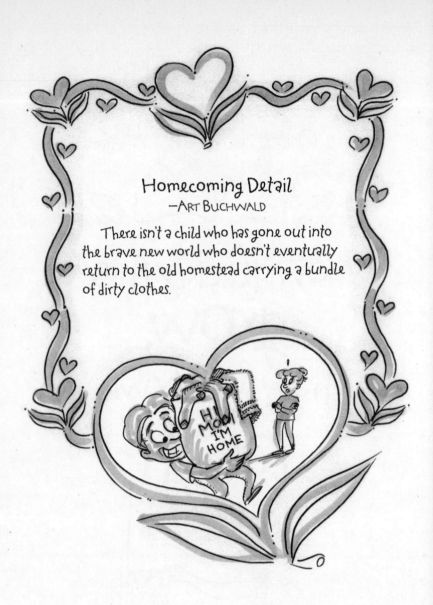

Homecoming Detail
—Art Buchwald

There isn't a child who has gone out into the brave new world who doesn't eventually return to the old homestead carrying a bundle of dirty clothes.

Growing Up in Slow-Mo

Martha Bolton

Children grow up fast these days. Hopefully, we'll remember to take the time to enjoy them each step of the way. But just so the transition into adulthood doesn't catch you totally by surprise, you'll know your children are growing up when:

- You find yourself still trying to convince them of the importance of a nap...only now it's to get them to turn down their radios so you can take yours.

- They still cry when you leave the house...only now it's because your wallet's going with you.

- They still like to eat every three hours...only now it's at smorgasbords.

- They still like dressing up in Mommy's or Daddy's clothes...only now they fit, and you don't get them back.

- But you really know your children are growing up when they still wave bye-bye to you...only now it's from the driver's seat of your car!

In the Throes of Mother Henhood

Becky Freeman

It was the perfect night for high school football—a beautiful October evening in Texas. The air was crisp, the band was playing something patriotic and snappy, and the Buffalos' red uniforms, contrasted with the blue shirts worn by the other team, looked so lovely against the green field. (We women notice those things.)

All was bright and beautiful until our son Zeke, a junior, went down on the football field and didn't get back up—every parent's nightmare.

As the paramedics rushed forward, my husband, Scott, took the bleacher steps two at a time, bounded over the tall fence, and rushed to our son. I ran along behind him, my heart in my throat. Then I came face to face with the fence. *What to do, what to do?* I stopped for a fleeting second and thought, *If I climb this*

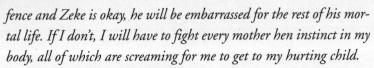

fence and Zeke is okay, he will be embarrassed for the rest of his mortal life. If I don't, I will have to fight every mother hen instinct in my body, all of which are screaming for me to get to my hurting child.

What can I say? I'm a Mom—I climbed.

When I got to the sidelines, Scott looked up and caught my eye, motioning for me to return to "the mother spot"—on the other side of the fence. "Dislocated elbow," he yelled. "Go get the car and meet us at the hospital with the insurance forms."

I retraced my steps, my legs feeling as though they belonged to a rubber chicken, then once again, I came to the fence. In the moments since I had valiantly tackled it—it had *grown!*

Nothing hurt
that night
but my heart.

Try as I might, I could not get over the thing, so the cheerleaders gathered around me in pyramid formation and shoved me up and over, where I landed in a heap and injured my own knee. A kind man and good friend helped me off the field and drove me to the hospital. (He also discreetly pointed out that there was a gate not five yards from where I'd taken my undignified tumble.)

My knee was terribly sprained, but I felt nothing until the next day—nothing hurt that night but my heart. Hobbling into the emergency room to see my son, I couldn't help noticing how beautiful and filthy he was, part little boy and part grown man.

"Mom?" he asked as he lay there with his arm outstretched and wrapped in splints, his eyes filled with pain—"why are *you* limping?"

I hopped on one leg until I was near enough to put my arms around him. "I'm fine," I said, "it's just a mother hen thing." He looked confused but I didn't explain as I leaned on the clean

white pillow, stroking and kissing his cheek. "And how are you, son?"

"I'll be okay, Mom," he said, his voice breaking only slightly, "God was with me."

I forget that sometimes. But what a comforting thought. I can't always be with my children. I can't always protect them, though the Lord knows how much I want to. The good news is that God's presence knows no bounds. He can be father, mother, friend, and brother to our kids—at least until we moms can waddle in and give them a kiss on the cheek.

Future Mothers of the Groom Wear Radar and Keep Their Eyes Peeled

Charlene Ann Baumbich

One blessing of being the mother of boys is that one day most of them will end up with a girl. You will finally have a family member who doesn't ask you why you need new lip gloss, or why you are crying *again,* or why you talk on the phone so much. (Okay, so Butch doesn't ask those questions either, and neither does my parakeet, but I have to scoop their poop, and that loses them lots of points.)

Or at least you *hope* you acquire a daughter-in-law. Or sometimes you hope you do, but please, please, oh please God, not this one! Or, God, if it is this one, help me remember that taste in clothes, entertainment, and annoying habits are not something by which to judge a person—nor, yippie skippie, are they hereditary. But that those gorgeous eyes and great hair and long legs (that I covet) are, and wouldn't they look swell on my grandkids?

Over the years my boys have been involved with an eclectic assortment of young ladies. The lovelies have worn hair of gold and hair of raven—and one had hair of many colors. There have been shy ones and noisy ones and those who didn't speak my language. Some I never met and some I wished I never had. Some sang in the choir and some arm wrestled, others wrestled in a big pool of JELL-O. (Okay, so it was the same person who did the unique and varied kinds of wrestling, but she made awesome mashed potatoes. And aren't we to find the good in everyone?)

Some have slipped right into my life and others scared me out of my wits, causing me to lose my beauty sleep and pray like a banshee. "Yes, God, you have my attention over this one."

Some of the breakups have been of the "Phew!" variety, from my sons' and my point of view, and some have broken our hearts, mother and child both.

A couple of breakups had me wondering if there shouldn't be a law forbidding kids from such an act until after they received permission from their mothers. If so, I would not have granted it because I had fallen in love with this girl who already seemed like my family. Nobody asked me if I was ready for it to end.

When my sons grew older and moved away, they sometimes brought their love interests home to meet the family during the holidays. Some of their love interests didn't travel well. No, not well at all. At least that's what the boys told us. They swore that kind of behavior had never been displayed before.

And how do you know when it's time to start buying the current love interest gifts? I began feeling like a jinx when, for the third time in a row, I bought a gift for someone my son was no longer dating by the time the holiday rolled around, and sometimes that was a very short gap. When I decided not to tempt fate in that way, the Ms. Wonderfuls were, of course, still around and showering me with delightful presents that made me feel like a loser because I had nothing with which to reciprocate.

You want to love the significant other because your child does; you don't want to see them plunge headlong into obvious disaster. You don't want to say anything bad about what you perceive to be a horrendous match. Neither do you want to hold your tongue and have them get on *Oprah* one day, saying they have been estranged from their mother and in counseling for twenty-five years because Mom never told them the truth. I can read the *TV Guide* already: *Sons who love psychotic women and whose mothers knew it all along, but didn't tell because they love their sons.*

You want them to chose someone like you because it would be so flattering. On the other hand, you're afraid they'll choose a better version of you, thereby wrecking your self-esteem and making you prime talk show fodder: *Mothers whose sons marry women just like them only better.*

You want them to be happy, even if you believe you might one day need to wear Mother of the Groom Leathers, because that seems to be the outfit of choice for both your son and his current cutie.

Then you finally get tired of trying to read the future, and decide to put it in God's hands. You take to heart the mother who said she began praying for her children's spouses the day her kids were born. In fact, she prayed for the parents of her children's spouses. And you wish you'd done the same.

But you decide to get off that fruitless guilt trip and, with all the spare time you save by not flogging yourself, you undertake

redecorating your kitchen. You find yourself choosing this very large and deep sink because you see your fat-cheeked little grandchild sitting down in the basin while you squirt them with the cleverly designed and very costly combination faucet/spray thingie.

I'm sure I had a dreamy glow on my face as I stood like Vanna in front of the vowels showing Brian our new sink and carrying on about his one-day little cherub, whom I pictured as having the best features of his parents and loving his grandmother to pieces.

Not long after telling Brian my dream, I was parting the hair on the side of my head to show him how much silver I was accumulating. (I don't dye my hair; I "color enhance the pigment-impaired parts.")

"I better hurry up with those grandkids!" he said.

"What?"

"I didn't know you were *that* old."

"Please, Brian. How about getting a girlfriend first? Then a wife? Then a child? A billion gray hairs are all I can handle right now."

No, son. Not to hurry. Don't pace your life or change your plans or make your choices on account of me. I mean it. Just think about all the guys I dated...

No son. Don't think about that. I mean it.

And don't pay any attention to the fact that I occasionally whip your photo out of my wallet and show it to someone who has just the right cheekbones and a kind heart and a bright smile and a giving spirit and who is available. Just in case you were looking. Just in case you wanted me to help you. Just in case God needs a hand. Just in case.

you've got to be kidding

—more family humor

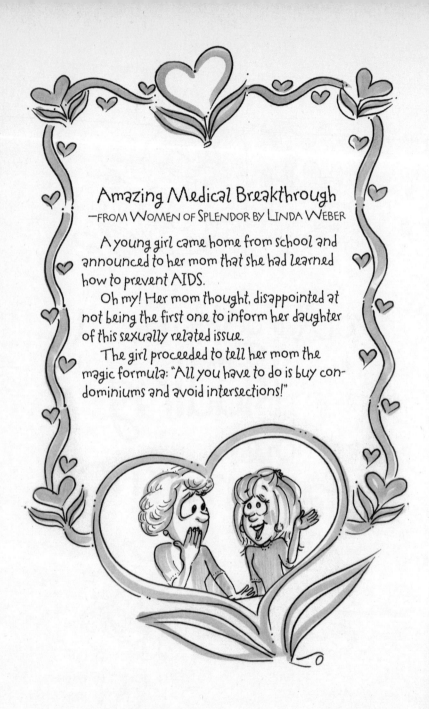

Amazing Medical Breakthrough
—FROM WOMEN OF SPLENDOR BY LINDA WEBER

A young girl came home from school and announced to her mom that she had learned how to prevent AIDS.

Oh my! Her mom thought, disappointed at not being the first one to inform her daughter of this sexually related issue.

The girl proceeded to tell her mom the magic formula: "All you have to do is buy condominiums and avoid intersections!"

Angels Don't Always Have Wings

Gwendolyn Mitchell Diaz

She was having a hard time buying me gifts. She never knew quite what to get me, so about five years ago, my sister-in-law decided that I needed to start an angel collection. She wrapped my first one and presented it to me that Christmas. It was a beautiful porcelain angel with long delicate wings. Ever since, she has continued to build me one of the most delightful, eclectic collections of angels one can imagine.

However, there was one thing my sister-in-law failed to take into consideration when she selected angels as the object of my accumulation—the fact that she has four, very active, often rowdy nephews who happen to live in my house!

That, and the fact that most angels are either fragile or frilly, has led to some very interesting moments. Teetering angels have barely been caught as they tipped from the top of the bookshelf. Ruffled,

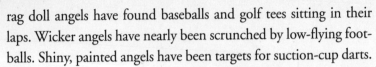

rag doll angels have found baseballs and golf tees sitting in their laps. Wicker angels have nearly been scrunched by low-flying footballs. Shiny, painted angels have been targets for suction-cup darts.

Miraculously, every angel has managed to survive each episode…until this morning, that is, which explains why I am typing this with my left hand while the thumb and index finger of my right hand remain interminably stuck together.

Following a wrestling match (which included all four of my sons and their father!), I found my tiniest angel cowering behind the television set, unable to fly back to its home. One of its miniature ceramic wings had been clipped completely off when a flailing limb had sent it flying.

> "Look, Mom glued herself together!"

Quite upset, I picked up the itsy pieces and stomped into the kitchen. I hunted in every messy drawer 'til I found the glue that guarantees it can put everything from Humpty Dumpty to china teapots back together again. The accompanying brochure mentions its special powers to bond paper, rubber, ceramics, leather, and wood.

It forgets to mention one thing: skin!

After two minutes of holding the pieces firmly in place, the only objects stuck together were my fingers. The angel was as wingless as it had been when it first struck the floor.

I approached my sons and tried to plead my case for a kinder, gentler household, but they were much too amused by my lack of gluing prowess to pay much attention.

"Look, Mom glued herself together!"

"I always knew you were stuck on yourself, Mom."

"Mom's just trying to get out of doing the dishes."

"Hey, Mom. What's the difference between an angel with one wing and an angel with two?" one of them quipped.

When I failed to respond, he said, "Not much. It's just a difference of a pinion. Ha, ha, ha. Get it? A *pinion!* That's a big word for a 'wing' in case you didn't know, Mom!"

I wasn't amused.

"Come on, Mom, smile. It's just a little ceramic angel. It's not like one of us got hurt or something."

He left the room and came back a few minutes later holding a perfectly glued, deceptively unflawed little angel. And all of his fingers were functioning quite normally.

He handed me the angel and reached over to kiss me on the cheek.

"Did you get it yet? A *pinion* instead of *opinion?*" he asked sheepishly, trying to make me smile.

He succeeded, and I realize…I have lots of angels. Some of them are just more rambunctious than others.

Stay Home–Alone

Marti Attoun

School field trips are a great learning experience. A parent/
chaperone gathers so much data on his first field trip that it often
takes him a week or two to recover and figure out everything he
learned. By his second or third trip, he's formulated and memo-
rized these five basic rules:

*1. What's off the beaten path is always more exciting than what's
on it.* During a 2nd-grade field trip to a local bakery, the company guide patiently led everyone through the step-by-step
recipe for a jillion ginger snaps. She showed off the mixers as big
as Volkswagens, the chute where all that dough shoots, the con-
veyor belt where the cookies ride out of the oven in endless
brown dots, and the machines that automatically bag and box
the cookies.

"Any questions?" she asked after 30 minutes of explanation.

"Yeah," one kid said, pointing to the fire escape. "Don't you guys get tired climbing all those steps every day?"

"How much does a Coke cost in that machine downstairs?" another hollered.

2. If it's edible, it will attract more attention than anything on a pedestal or in a showcase. During a tour of the newsroom where I worked, a reporter showed off the computers and up-to-the-minute stories from around the world. Another explained about laser photos.

"Wow," a kid said as he looked at my screen. I smiled. I thought I was writing a pretty good story, too.

"Look at that chocolate doughnut this lady has," he said. Another kid ran over and checked out our desktop displays: "No fair. This one over here even has a bag of popcorn."

"Look at that chocolate dough-nut this lady has."

3. The journey is always more thrilling than the destination. I listened to the account of my son's hospital field trip. I expected to hear about the sophisticated, million-dollar lifesaving equipment and disease-detecting devices. I thought he might be inspired to become a doctor—or at least be scared into some healthy habits, like quitting Junior Mints cold turkey.

"On the bus, Nick's mother showed us how to make a paper frog," he said. "But then we had to get off the bus and go through that boring hospital."

4. During the question period, always expect something basic and personal. "How much do you guys get paid to work here?" a

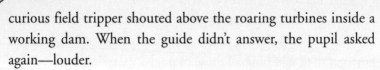

curious field tripper shouted above the roaring turbines inside a working dam. When the guide didn't answer, the pupil asked again—louder.

"Not nearly enough!" the guide finally shot back.

5. The souvenir will always add a creative dimension to the return trip. On one trip, so many freebie company pencils and brochures took flight that a father/chaperone had a hands-on experience and confiscated them. He learned a lesson that day: Stay home next time.

When You Gotta Go

Renae Bottom

It was supposed to be the perfect antidote for a months-long crescendo of frazzled-parent burnout. It was supposed to be a long, relaxing road trip, alone with my husband, Mark. It was *not* supposed to be the Olympic trials for bladder control.

I had anticipated this get-away excursion with all the desperation of a working mother on the brink. The morning of the departure, I brewed a pot of coffee and mentally rehearsed our trip. The children were safe at my sister's. There would be no negotiations with our three-year-old son over what constituted "finishing" a bologna sandwich; no arguments with our nine-year-old daughter over whether bangs as big as tidal waves were appropriate coiffure for third-grade girls.

Today, I would be an adult. I poured another cup of coffee, and my fantasy unfolded like a Lexus commercial. I was cruising

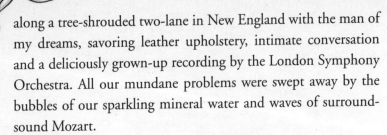

along a tree-shrouded two-lane in New England with the man of my dreams, savoring leather upholstery, intimate conversation and a deliciously grown-up recording by the London Symphony Orchestra. All our mundane problems were swept away by the bubbles of our sparkling mineral water and waves of surround-sound Mozart.

Never mind that we were really just an average husband and wife, deserting our comfortable bed before dawn to slip into K-mart sweats and strike off across eastern Wyoming in a used minivan. I had already booked passage on the fantasy.

As we loaded the van, I took a deep breath and commented on the fresh, cold tingle of the pre-dawn air. Mark hummed a tune and happily commented that we could get 25 miles to the gallon if we'd set the cruise on 65 and keep the van moving.

I should have seen disaster coming.

The first 30 minutes of the trip we almost managed to re-member what adults talk about. Then my early-morning coffee caught up with me. "Let's stop here," I said, pointing to a small, roadside gas station.

"Already?" Mark checked his watch and raised one eyebrow, but patiently pulled over.

"I won't be long," I promised. "I ran in for a quick rest stop and bought a fresh cup of coffee for each of us. We headed back onto the open road—for all of 30 more minutes.

"But we just stopped," Mark protested, as he parked the van at a truck plaza. I could see the record-keeping whiz I married, mentally calculating our loss in gas mileage.

Two more truck plazas and one convenience store later, my nervous bladder was proving a serious antidote to fantasy. The

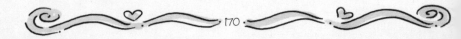

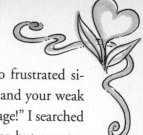

intimate conversation I'd imagined devolved into frustrated silence after a heated exchange about "you women and your weak
bladders!" and "you men and your stupid gas mileage!" I searched
for a classical station on the radio; I found nothing but country
and western.

When nature called again, I couldn't bear to tell Mark.
Requesting yet another pit stop on this fascinating tour of
Wyoming's restrooms might well result
in my hitchhiking the remaining miles
to Cheyenne.

I decided I could wait. After all,
Mark had been drinking his share of
coffee. Surely he'd have to stop soon. I
vowed to outlast him.

Was the man
superhuman?
Would he never
require the use of
a bathroom?

One by one, the miles slipped past
my window. One by one, opportunities for relief slipped past
with them. There was a rest stop coming up on the right, and it
looked almost sanitary. Surely Mark would pull in. There was a
gas station with a sign that said "Restrooms Inside"—surely
Mark would stop.

But he just kept driving. I crossed my legs and stole a glance
in his direction. Was the man superhuman? Would he never require the use of a bathroom? For a moment, I thought I detected
a slightly deeper-than-usual furrow of concentration on his brow,
but I couldn't be sure. Was he trying to outlast me? I wouldn't
give him the satisfaction.

Ten minutes later, I caught myself eyeing an isolated grove of
trees with unnatural longing. I knew I couldn't hold out much
longer. "Why don't we stop at the next convenience store?" I

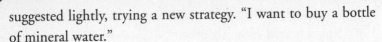

suggested lightly, trying a new strategy. "I want to buy a bottle of mineral water."

Mark shot me a quick look. Was that suspicion or anticipation I saw in his eyes? I couldn't think about it now. Once we stopped, I would give him the slip and sneak into the bathroom. He'd never have to know.

We parked the van, and I struggled to walk normally toward the front door. Once inside, I ducked behind the potato chip aisle and sprinted the last 50 feet to the restroom. When I emerged, I noticed the door marked "MEN" swinging shut behind my husband. He quickly looked both ways, then ambled toward the drink coolers.

> Something in my
> upbringing kept
> my hands from
> closing around
> his throat.

No sparkling mineral water in sight, we paid for our snacks and got back in the van. "So how long did you have to go to the bathroom before we finally stopped," I asked, as we pulled back onto the highway.

The growing mischief in Mark's smile told me all I needed to know. "I didn't really have to go," he said. "I was just being efficient—as long as we were stopped anyway."

Something in my upbringing kept my hands from closing around his throat. I weighed my options, then calmly rolled up the largest map in the glove compartment and began whapping the man of my dreams with it. One arm up to fend off my attack, Mark reminded me that the driving patterns inspired by such antics are frowned upon by those who patrol our nation's interstate highways.

I ceased and desisted, but only after a few more well-aimed shots. By that time we were both laughing so hard any further at-

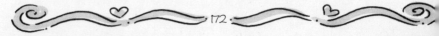

tempt at retribution was futile. After we regained our composure, we finally succeeded in having that grown-up talk I had longed for—over sunflower seeds and Cokes, while the country-and-western classic "The Streets of Laredo" played softly in the background.

I realized then, as we cruised through the east-Wyoming countryside, that I liked our style, even it if meant we'd be the last couple chosen for a Lexus ad. And a few miles down the road, when we passed another truck plaza, it was Mark who suggested we pull in for a pit stop.

14

mother, may i laugh?

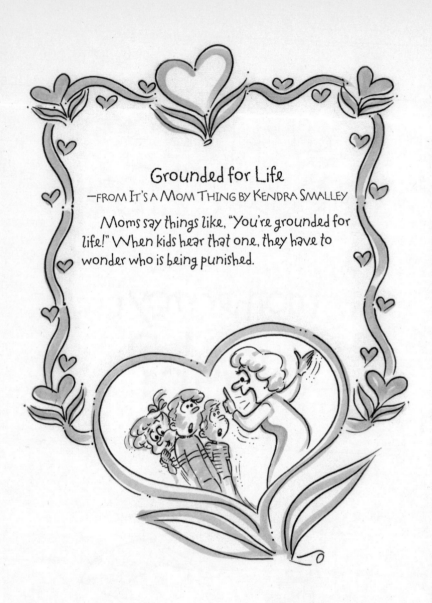

Grounded for Life
—FROM IT'S A MOM THING BY KENDRA SMALLEY

Moms say things like, "You're grounded for life!" When kids hear that one, they have to wonder who is being punished.

Learning to Land

Gwendolyn Mitchell Diaz

He was tiny—maybe four years old—when he came to me and asked for a Superman cape. With very little money available for the purchase of such frivolities, I fashioned one from an old blanket and fastened it around my son's shoulders.

He was thrilled! Off he zoomed, running around and around the house, jumping off beds, chairs, couches—anything high enough to be challenging and sturdy enough to hold his two little feet. Always his cape flowed behind him, flapping in the wake of his breakneck pace. It was when he decided to leap from the dining table onto the kitchen countertop, across the sink, and up onto the refrigerator that I figured it was time for him to head outdoors.

As I watched him carefully from the window, he ran at top speed and flung himself into the air across an embankment

which separated our house from our neighbors'. Over and over he ran his fastest, leaped with his arms outstretched, and kicked his feet out behind him. Over and over he landed smack on his belly and took a huge bite out of our neighbor's sod. Over and over he dusted himself off, rearranged his cape, and tried again,

> It was Matthew, poised and ready for a leap of true Superman proportions.

fully expecting to take flight. I cringed every time he landed, but he didn't seem to be in great danger of breaking any bones or dislodging teeth. I figured that before long he would tire of the futile attempts and come back inside with a little less energy to spare.

I became distracted with the busyness of caring for the other children. When I next glanced out the window, my attention was drawn to a bright, blue blob at the very tip-top of the highest orange tree in our side yard. It was Matthew, poised and ready for a leap of true Superman proportions.

I flung open the window and yelled, "MattE, NO! Don't jump. Wait for Mommy!" I ran outside and used every adult psychological technique I could think of to coax him down from his precarious perch. I even resorted to bribery and the promise of milk and cookies.

Once he was on solid ground, the cape was removed and promptly hidden. We sat down for our promised snack and a discussion of the danger of climbing trees—including the consequences that would follow if he ever tried such a thing again.

"You shouldn't worry about me, Mommy," Matthew insisted as he dunked a cookie in his plastic cup, splashing milk all over the table. "I've learned to land real good when my cape doesn't work. This one you gave me doesn't have a real lot of power, you know."

It's probably something Superman never had to consider, but learning to land "real good" when your cape doesn't work is an important part of life for us humans. Now, some fourteen years later, Matthew is about to take the biggest leap of his life as he leaves home and heads to college. We've created a cape for him over the years, one designed from many lessons and lots of love. And we've invested this one with special power, the power of prayer.

There are times, because he is human, that Matt's cape won't work. Hopefully we've provided enough opportunities for him over the years to learn to land "real good" on his own. That way, when it does fail him, he can dust himself off with God's grace and love, rearrange his cape, and try again.

The Fish Pond
Carolyn Arends

If for some mysterious reason you wanted to shoot a documentary about my life, and you had to set the entire film in one location, the obvious choice would be Blue Mountain Park. It was the official Jonat family park (Jonat is my maiden name, which you should know if you're making a documentary about me) from the time I was a toddler until we moved away just before my sixth birthday. We returned to the neighborhood—the prodigal family—when I was twelve, and we have played happily in the sun-dappled shadows of its massive pine trees ever since.

The far side of the woods opens out into a clearing, a stretch of reasonably level lawn perfectly suited for the throwing of frisbees and the staging of three-legged races. Picnic tables are scattered around the periphery, making this location ideal for Sunday

school picnics. The good people of Blue Mountain Baptist Church have been spending greasy Sunday afternoons eating Kentucky Fried Chicken here for dozens of years, and I have often been a part of the happy throng. For the purposes of the documentary, you could edit in a couple of photographs I took after church one Sunday just last summer. There is a wide shot of the baseball diamond—boys skinning their knees and men pulling their muscles in an impromptu but impassioned game of softball. And in another picture there are half a dozen children, including a very drenched and delighted Ben, splashing about the water park (which, although I haven't even mentioned it yet, is fabulous) under the watchful eyes of Jennifer, Jackie, Elise, Kristy, and Megan—the helpful older girls who sometimes mind the kids so the women can talk.

None of those kids (and only a few of the women) know that there used to be a fish pond over on the other side of the woods. It was replaced with the much more exciting water park long ago, sometime during the six-and-a-half years I was living too far away to protest. But Chris and I can both remember the pond distinctly. It was constructed with flat heavy stones and mortar, shaped like a sawed-off above-ground swimming pool, and filled with endlessly fascinating orange and brown fish. Our mother must have taken us there dozens of times. But there is one particular visit that has become the stuff of family legend, and it is the most indelible of all my Blue Mountain Park memories.

I was four, maybe five at the oldest; Chris was two or three. It was the early '70s, so there was undoubtedly a good deal of polyester involved. My dad was at work, my mom was with us. We had played hard in the kiddie park, run through the woods,

chased a few stray tennis balls, and stopped by the snack stand for grape Popsicles. We were only a short trip to the fish pond away from a perfect day at the park.

When we arrived at the pond, we were the only three visitors, so we felt especially free to chat with the fish, sing them silly songs, and engage in various other eccentric Jonat rituals. But my mother noticed right away that something was wrong. "Look!" she gasped, with genuine horror. "There is litter in the fish pond." We realized with a shock that it was true—some unimaginably derelict individual had sullied the water with a candy wrapper. If my memory is accurate, the trash was from an Oh Henry! chocolate bar.

> Some unimaginably derelict individual had sullied the water with a candy wrapper.

Without hesitating, my mother began to climb up the rocky side of the fish pond. "Children," she said, panting a little with the exertion, "when we see litter like this, we have a chance to make the world a better place." She was balancing on the edge of the pond, and each time she reached out to grab the wrapper, a mischievous breeze blew it just a little out of reach. "Cleaning up garbage is simple," she exclaimed virtuously, shifting positions to try to get closer to the offending item, "and yet it makes such a big difference." We were nodding encouragingly, fully in support of the initiative to make the world a better place for the fish. "Remember," said my mother triumphantly, just as she finally got a good hold of the wrapper and began to drag it out, "it's up to us to do the right thing!"

And then she fell in.

We were terrified. She was lying face down in the water, and she

was shaking. "Mom!" cried Chris. The fish—who appeared to be quite agitated—were radiating out and away from her body in every direction. "Help!" I shouted. No one came. It seemed certain that our mother was about to drown in six inches of pond water.

We were as relieved as we were confused when she finally managed to roll over and it became apparent that she was shaking with—of all things—*laughter*. Her favorite orange and green rayon pantsuit was torn, and her beehive hairdo had collapsed inwardly, so that it looked like a water-filled flowerpot. She was bleeding from several different locations. And, inexplicably, she was still laughing with a mirth so pure it was contagious. Chris and I laughed, too, although we were a little bewildered and quite anxious to get our mother out of the fish pond.

After several failed attempts, she managed to hurl her wounded self back onto dry land. She rested and bled a few moments on the grass, and then she stood up, ceremoniously dropped the candy wrapper into the nearest trash receptacle, took each of her children by the hand, and limped bravely and soggily home—laughing all the way.

In twenty-odd years of hanging around Blue Mountain Park—cheering in its bleachers, losing on its tennis courts, falling onto leaves and into love on its wooded paths, fellowshipping with various saints at its picnic tables, and chasing my son over every blessed green inch—I have learned a few things. Play hard. Watch for birds and airplanes and other miracles through the trees. Pick up litter. Try to make the world a better place. And if you should fall—if you should find yourself bloodied and looking and feeling ridiculous—don't forget to laugh.

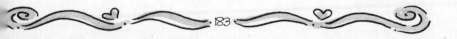

Acrylic Nail Tip Adventures

Renae Bottom

One Saturday night, in a frenzy of female bonding, my 11-year-old daughter convinced me to try do-it-yourself nail tips.

Generally speaking, I'm not a nail-tips sort of person. But on this particular night the guys were gone, we had the house to ourselves, and we'd eaten just enough chocolate-chip cookie dough to be dangerous.

Giggling like a couple of kids at a slumber party, we drove to the local drugstore and purchased all the supplies necessary for creating salon-quality nails at home.

My daughter had been playing with press-on nails for years, so she agreed to act as my coach. I'm decidedly challenged in the area of "salon quality," so I needed all the help I could get.

We began by spreading our nail-building arsenal on the kitchen counter. Out of the boxes tumbled a frightening assort-

ment of unnatural-looking utensils. Each item looked like something created in a pink, plastic laboratory by Mad Scientist Barbie.

There were two bushels of fake nails, in assorted sizes. A miniature bottle of super-bond glue, designed for use by Munchkins. Liquid acrylic nail gel, more aptly referred to as Quick-Set Cement in a Bottle. And a mysterious assortment of emery pads and ceremonial wooden sticks, apparently intended for grinding and poking one's natural nails into a condition conducive to the application of Quick-Set Cement in a Bottle.

The needle on my Internal Fortitude Meter took a gigantic swing toward Common Sense. I gazed on this mystifying mountain of nail paraphernalia and immediately suggested that we sweep the whole mess into the trash and start a good movie.

My daughter insisted that I couldn't be a quitter. She pointed out how wasteful it would be to throw away good money on a project we never even attempted.

Suitably shamed, I agreed to proceed with our experiment. So began an ordeal that would become a full-length, salon-quality nightmare.

Starting with my left thumb, I buffed, trimmed, filed, poked, sanded, and successfully applied a nail tip. Through a clever mishandling of the super glue, I also successfully bonded my right thumb to my right index finger.

Fifteen failed remedies later, I decided there were worse things than going through life with two fingers permanently joined. A long soak in warm water, mixed with nail polish remover, finally released the glue's stubborn grip. I dried my throbbing fingers and resolutely pronounced the experiment over.

My daughter, ever the optimist, cheerfully pointed out how

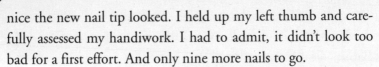

nice the new nail tip looked. I held up my left thumb and carefully assessed my handiwork. I had to admit, it didn't look too bad for a first effort. And only nine more nails to go.

If I hadn't eaten quite so much cookie dough, I might have realized that nine more nails, at thirty minutes each, amounted to a bedtime somewhere between 4 A.M. and dawn's early light.

By midnight my daughter was fast asleep in the recliner. I was flying solo, with five more nails to go. A thoroughly right-handed individual, I hadn't counted on how difficult the buffing, trimming, filing, poking, and sanding procedure would be once I reversed the procedure and used my left hand to work on my right.

I fumbled with the tiny utensils, growing more and more frustrated with every tick of the clock. Exhausted, increasingly cross-eyed, I resolved to work faster, thus hastening the end of my torture. Ah, what folly I reaped by combining haste with Quick-Set Cement in a Bottle.

> What folly I reaped by combining haste with Quick-Set Cement in a Bottle.

By the time I finished, my right hand looked like it had fallen off the Creature from the Black Lagoon and been reattached to the end of my arm. (Except that in my case, the monster emerged from the murky swamp sporting "Springtime Coral" on its hideous claws.)

It was far too late to remove the foul things, and I certainly didn't possess the expertise for fixing them. I went to church that morning with both hands firmly planted in my pockets.

I'm happy to report that the nail tips came off that afternoon, although it took several days to chip the last of the super-bond glue from my cuticles.

My daughter reassured me that the whole ordeal had been a learning experience. After all, half my nails had turned out reasonably well. I assured her that this learning experience would be our last foray into the world of do-it-yourself beauty science.

Acrylic nail tips may be the latest fashion fad, but they give me a sensation I can only describe as claustrophobia of the hands. I'll stick with my own humble, stubby nails, thank you, and leave the glamorous kind for those women whose hands never dip below the surface of their dirty dishwater.

I threw away the mountain of manicure tools, taking care to destroy all the evidence of my late-night crimes against cosmetology.

I did hang on to one souvenir. I kept the Quick-Set Cement in a Bottle. I'm not nostalgic about my failed experiment with nail tips, but I figure the stuff might come in handy someday, if a fender ever falls off my car.

ignorance is (domestic) bliss

Excuses, Excuses
—FROM THE NEW MESSIES MANUAL
BY SANDRA FELTON

Excuse (ik-'skyüs) n. A perfectly reasonable explanation for the fact that your husband can't find the monthly bills...or the checkbook...or one pen that hasn't gone dry because someone left the top off for two weeks.

Life's Grind
(A Man's View of Ironing)

Tim Wildmon

Mountain, be thou removed.

"Mountain, be thou removed.

"Mountain, be THOU removed."

I barely opened one eye. The mountain was still there. I continued.

"Okay. Last chance, mountain. Be thou removed...please."

The mountain called my bluff.

"What are you doing?" Alison said as she walked into our bedroom.

"Well, baby, I've had it with ironing. I was hoping that if I prayed hard enough the Lord would take this mountain of clothing from me," I responded.

As a man of the nineties, ironing, like life's daily grind, is always before me. Life is hard sometimes. And I realize I have it

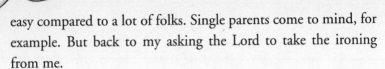

easy compared to a lot of folks. Single parents come to mind, for example. But back to my asking the Lord to take the ironing from me.

"You ever heard the phrase 'taking the Bible out of context,' Tim?"

"Well, yeah, but let me ask you a question 'in context.' Who came up with this idea of ironing anyway? What makes pressed shirts any better than wrinkled shirts? Think about it. Wrinkled is a shirt's natural state, no? It appears to me someone with nothing better to do came along and invented what we now call an iron and duped millions of people into thinking they have to have one."

> I see my iron as a partner in this labor camp I call home.

"Well, you're entitled to your wild speculations, I suppose, but you're going to burn a hole in your shirt if you don't quit talkin' and get that iron off," Alison said as she nodded her head toward the ironing board and folded a towel.

Yes, ladies and gentlemen, for the most part, I do the ironing in this family. Now I know what you're thinking. You're thinking, *What a waste of intellectual dynamite that, if harnessed, and not wasted on time spent ironing, could change the face of the world as we know it and lead to peace, understanding, and goodwill among peoples of all races, creeds, and nationalities.* Well, I'm thinking somewhat the same thing, but more along the lines of watching a little more basketball *in addition to* fostering peace, understanding, and goodwill among peoples of all races, creeds, and nationalities.

Seeing that I iron almost every night, I have a few fine points of pressing etiquette I like to follow. One is *I like to always have*

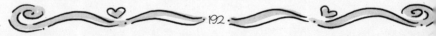

the iron turned on when I use it. This is very important. You've done it—started pressing only to discover there's no heat, no steam, to get the wrinkles out. Again, the first step to a successful pressing experience: Turn iron on.

Second, I like steam to come out of my Sunbeam 2000 (I added the 2000 because it just sounds more masculine) and I want it accompanied by the customary noise an iron makes when it gives off steam. *Shhhhhhahah* is basically how it sounds. I love that sound. I often say this back to my iron: "Shhhhhhhahah the man!" I say in response. In human relationships, this is called bonding. I'm basically saying to my little household appliance friend, "You and me, bud. I'll push, you keep steaming, I'll give you water and let you up for air every few minutes and yes, indeed, we'll conquer this mass of cotton and nylon, together, by midnight." And my iron calls back to me, "Shhhhhhhahah, master! We shall indeed overcome."

Although generally thought of as an inanimate object, for me at least, it's important that I see my iron as a partner in this labor camp I call home, much like an old farmer may have bonded with his mule. We sweat together. We take on pleats with a passion not unlike a farmer and mule taking on hardened soil. (Alison has adopted a "don't ask, don't tell" policy with me on this "relationship." As long as I get the ironing done, she cares not about what motivational techniques I utilize to accomplish the task. I admire her for not feeling threatened.)

I am constantly making sure the water level is where I can see it. I can't stand to dry iron. Don't ask me why; it's just one of my little quirks. The other night my water level was getting dangerously low which—for me—means I can't see water in the little clear window. If you can't see the water, you're getting way too close to dry ironing for my comfort zone. It's like driving a car long after your gas gauge has been below the red area. So I went to the bathroom to get a cup of water and discovered a glass already filled with water. I assumed someone had gotten a drink and had just left what remained in the cup. So, I—ever the conservationist—took it over to the iron and poured it all in and continued to iron. This was a big mistake, I would quickly learn. It wasn't but a couple of minutes and my trusty little Sunbeam began making terrible, strange noises and spitting the water back out its spout. It was the weirdest ironing experience I've ever had, and I, my friends, am an ironing veteran of many years. I have been around the ironing block a few times. I've seen a lot, but nothing to prepare me for this.

"Alison, come back here and look at this baby," I yelled up front and then stood back in amazement. For some reason, my little household appliance friend was turning on me. It was in utter rebellion, just spraying and sputtering. It was bucking on the board. It turned ugly. Occasionally, little brown dots of water would come forth in volcanic fashion. Then, to make things worse, it began emitting an awful odor. It smelled strangely like burnt sugar.

"What in the world have you done to my iron?" Alison said as she entered the room, looked at me, and then back at the iron. I stepped back farther from the machine to watch this twilight-zone spectacle.

"I ain't done nothin'," I said in good around-the-house Southern English. "I just got the cup of water from the bathroom and poured it in the iron and it started having a fit."

"You didn't get the cup beside the sink, did you?"

"Well, yeah. It was full of water. What's the deal?"

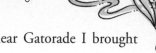

"No, no, baby. That's the cup of clear Gatorade I brought back here for Walker this afternoon."

"Oh."

"I just bought that iron. Couldn't you tell it wasn't water?"

This, readers, is what's known as a rhetorical question. Rhetorical questions are usually asked in frustration or to make the one being questioned admit he is an idiot.

My trusty little Sunbeam began making terrible, strange noises and spitting the water back out its spout.

Now, to me, ironing is a metaphor for life. And we all have our own private metaphors for life, don't we? For some it's farming. For others, flying kites. Whatever yours is, I'm not here to judge it. I simply ask that you respect mine: ironing. How so, you ask? Well, God has blessed me with a wonderful life. I have a beautiful wife, three healthy children, and a good job. And so many other blessings. So I'm not complaining. But still, like that perpetual pile of clothing in the basket that greets me each evening, the everyday routine of life—the daily grind, I call it—is always there. And this grind, well, it can wear me down sometimes. My body gets tired. My mind gets tired. My soul gets tired. It catches up with all of us from time to time, doesn't it? Raising children, doing an honest day's work at the office, church activities, domestic chores, paying bills, et cetera, takes a toll on the average American adult. And it's easy to get these priorities out of order. (That is, of course, if we can find time to get them out of order.)

It is both unreasonable and unrealistic to expect God to make life easy for us. The Bible promises no such escape. But the Lord does promise His children that He is with them all the time—

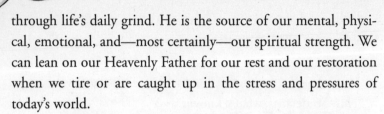

through life's daily grind. He is the source of our mental, physical, emotional, and—most certainly—our spiritual strength. We can lean on our Heavenly Father for our rest and our restoration when we tire or are caught up in the stress and pressures of today's world.

Jesus put it this way in Matthew 11:28–30 (NIV): "Come to me, all you who are weary and burdened, and I will give you rest. Take my yoke upon you and learn from me, for I am gentle and humble in heart, and you will find rest for your souls. For my yoke is easy and my burden is light."

As for my iron, it still stinks. As does ironing, for that matter. All I can say is, "Shhhhhhhhhahah! I will press on."

Wish I Were Crafty

Renae Bottom

I wish I were crafty. Not sly and clever, but craft-y, the sort of person who could create decorative wall art from ordinary household objects, like juice-can lids and broken chopsticks.

Unfortunately, I developed my full craft intelligence by age ten and I haven't advanced a bit since then. Pipe-cleaner creations, macaroni collage, construction paper cut-outs—these projects are about my speed. Adult materials like silk flowers and satin ribbon leave me at a loss.

Some talented individuals can take a few silk daisies, glue them to a tarnished candelabra, and create a centerpiece worthy of Martha Stewart. I can take a few silk daisies, glue them to a tarnished candelabra, and create something worthy of Lenny and Squiggy.

My hands understand weeding gardens. They understand washing dishes and scrubbing sinks. They even understand splicing broken shoelaces and fishing Tonka parts out of the garbage disposal. But they do not comprehend coaxing twenty-tier bows from a handful of curly ribbon, or painting cute smiles on wooden cows.

Still, I'm fascinated by craft supplies. I wander the aisles in craft stores, admiring the tiny beads, the smooth wooden boxes, the beautifully braided wreaths, just waiting for some creative soul to transform them into tasteful works of art.

"I wonder who glued moss to that old milk carton?"

I often bring home craft supplies. I purchase yarn and plastic berries, gingham ribbon and tiny ceramic figures. I don't make anything with the stuff. I just haul it out and look at it every few months, dreaming of what I might create if I could be trusted with a glue gun.

Even though I know my limitations, I was nearly inspired to begin a craft project one warm spring day, not long ago. The pattern called for cutting windows in a cardboard milk carton, then gluing moss and miniature flowers to the outside in order to create a birdhouse.

The finished example was adorable, but my craft projects don't turn out like the pictures in magazines.

If I hung my newly-finished creation in the front yard, no one would walk by and say, "Look at the adorable birdhouse." They'd be more likely to scratch their heads and say, "I wonder who glued moss to that old milk carton?"

And the sparrows? They'd laugh so hard, they'd fall out of the trees. Then they'd call in the blue jays and the finches, so they could laugh too. Before long, half the bird kingdom would be rolling in my front yard, overcome by hysterics at my attempt to create a habitat fit for creatures with wings and feathers.

I'm better off recycling my milk cartons and leaving the development of urban housing for birds to those more qualified for the job.

I'm afraid I'll be forever destined to appreciate beautiful crafts, but not to create them. I'll stick to my pipe cleaners and macaroni collages. When winter comes, I might even get daring and cut a few snowflakes from white paper.

Perhaps one day I'll awaken to discover that I've developed a sudden aptitude for crafts, but I'm not holding my breath. Until that day, I'll keep doing the projects that match my developmental level. And I'll keep insisting that the construction paper cut-outs on my refrigerator belong to the kids, and not to their mother.

Hen Hugs and Heart Tugs

Fran Caffey Sandin

The phone rang as I measured ingredients for a batch of brownies. I grabbed the dishtowel, wiped my hands, and lifted the receiver. "Hello?"

"Hi, Fran. This is Brenda. The booster club needs another pan of chicken enchiladas for the concession stand tonight. Can you help us?" Before I could reply, the faint ding-dong of the doorbell sounded through the hallway.

"Brenda, can you hold? Someone's at my front door." Still wearing my apron, I ran to the front where I greeted Mr. Watson.

"Here are the brooms and cleaning supplies you ordered, Mrs. Sandin. Where would you like me to leave them?" Pointing to a corner in the entry, I apologized, excused myself, and raced back to the kitchen.

"Oh, sure, Brenda," I panted. "I'll work it in."

Cutting our conversation short, I trotted back to the front, paid Mr. Watson, and stashed my cleaning supplies in the closet. On my way back to the kitchen, I detoured to the utility room to place a load of clothes in the washer. *Wow, I'm really getting things done today!* I thought as I sorted the clothes into piles, loaded the machine, twirled the knob, and flew out of the utility room.

I raced back to the kitchen and stared at my brownie mix thoughtfully. *Did I or did I not add baking powder? Yes? No? Oh, I don't remember. I'll add a little more,* I reasoned. *Better to rise too much than to fall flat.*

After scooting the pan into the oven, I plucked a frozen chicken from the freezer, thawed it in the microwave, and began preparing the enchiladas. The aroma of home-baked chocolate brownies drifted through the house as I darted back and forth pitching clothes from the washer to the dryer.

As I popped open the dryer door to empty the final load, something strange fell out. *Where did that cute little baby sweater come from?* I wondered. The hot pink texture had a think, spongy feel. Then it hit me. "Oh no! It can't be!" I squealed. "What on earth have I done?"

Angie at thirteen and supersensitive about her appearance, had one favorite sweater she treasured above all her other clothes. Each time she wore "the sweater" her friends showered her with compliments. Needless to say, Angie loved the attention and wore her prized possession at every opportunity.

Now the wool garment—never intended to see the inside of a washing machine—had shrunk to the size of one of her favorite stuffed animals—Snoopy—and it smelled like a real animal had been wearing it!

My knees felt weak and shaky and my heart raced as I considered

my very limited options. I knew Angie would be crushed and angry. I just didn't know which would come first. While wondering if I should confess or let her find it for herself, I realized how hilarious it looked. I began smiling and then broke into fits of laughter. However, within my mother hen heart, I knew my little chick-a-dee would not be amused.

I took a deep breath when I heard Angie close the car door and bounce into the kitchen.

"Mom, what smells soooooooooo good? Wow! Those brownies are huge! May I have one?" she asked while reaching for a square. Her roller-coaster emotions in high gear, Angie nibbled on a brownie, and chatted about the big game and the party plans afterwards. Then she paused and assumed a dramatic flair.

"Mother," she said dreamily, her eyes glistening, "Doug may ask me to sit with him tonight and I want to wear my pink sweater—you know it's the best looking thing I own."

I'd heard about hot flashes. Now I had one. Picking up a magazine, I fanned my flushing face. "Angie," I began tremulously, "I'm afraid there's been a little accident." As I slipped into the utility room to retrieve the tragic remains, I braced myself for the explosion and prayed quietly under my breath, "Dear Lord, help us all."

Recognition triggered the first outburst. Angie grabbed the pot-holder sized garment from my hands, held it up, looked at me with a serious, horrified expression, and exclaimed, "No way!" After a short pause, her alto voice became a high soprano as she squealed, "Mutheeeeeerrrrrrrrr! What did you do to my sweater?"

"I'm so sorry, Angie," I said softly. "I accidentally washed it with a load of towels. Wool sweaters have to be dry cleaned. Please forgive me. I promise to buy you a new sweater."

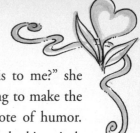

"Muuuthhheeeerrrrrr! How could you do this to me?" she howled. By this time we were both in tears. Trying to make the best of a bad situation, I decided to inject a note of humor. "Angie," I said cautiously, "I know it's not what you had in mind, but have you thought how cute Snoopy would look in that sweater?"

"MUTHERRRR!" she sobbed. "How could you even think such a thing at a time like this?"

"I'm so sorry, honey," I apologized. "Mothers are weird sometimes." With my place firmly secured in *The Guinness Book of Mama's Big Boo Boos,* I exited briskly before things got worse.

. . . ♥ . . .
I'd heard about
hot flashes.
Now I had one.

Later that afternoon, Angie recovered enough to find an alternative to "the sweater." She went to the game, the party, and Doug even asked her to sit with him. (Thank you, Jesus.) Within a few days, we were able to talk and laugh about the disaster. I replaced the original sweater with another pink one. (But I'll have to admit, it never had quite the pizzazz of the first.)

The sweater incident was only one of many times Angie and I clashed during her growing-up years, but we always found a way to mend our broken fences with forgiveness and lots of hugs. When Angie graduated from high school and left for college, a part of me departed, too. As I sat at home, sewing curtains for Angie's dorm room, I cried—not tears of sadness, not tears of happiness. Just a mother's heartfelt longing to hear her daughter's voice, to see her playing dolls, to watch her leading cheers, to feel her warm embrace.

Suddenly the collage of good times and bad times was framed by a special sweetness I could not appreciate while in the middle

of the fray. The stormy times took on poignant significance as I thought, *Angie has taught me so much about living life with passion, and about learning patience and practicing unconditional love. (Even how to do the laundry!)*

Through the years, Angie and I have developed a close, loving, and very special relationship. We converse with ease and express ourselves openly and honestly. My little girl is married to a wonderful young man and has become the mother of Emily Grace, our first grandchild. As I recently watched Angie feeding her own baby daughter, I felt a strong heart tug, almost as though it was reaching across the generations of time.

As I cuddled Emily, stroked her velvet skin, and smelled her fresh baby powder fragrance, I thought, *Lord, thank you for a double blessing.* Then I lifted Emily's downy head next to mine and whispered in her ear, "Now wouldn't you look smashing in that little hot pink sweater? Too bad I didn't save it!"

16

to mom,
with *love*
and *laughs*

It's a Grapefruit Day
—FROM ONE HUNDRED ONE UPWARD GLANCES
BY SANDRA P. ALDRICH

You know it's going to be a bad day when your four-year-old announces that it's almost impossible to flush a grapefruit.

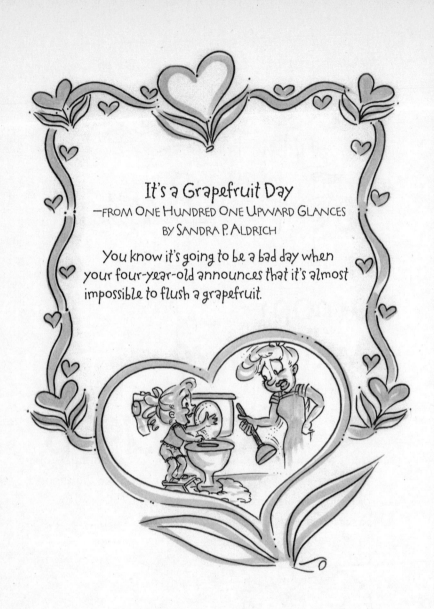

Curbin' Their Wormin' Ways

Becky Freeman with Ruthie Arnold

Everybody knows that children must be disciplined. That is, everyone except the children. What parent has not faced down the toddler who declares through his outthrust bottom lip, "You not the boss of me!" Then ensues a scene not unlike the shootout from *High Noon*. Hopefully, Mom is the one left standing.

Now, discipline has never been my strong suit, partly because of my Erma Bombeck vow to try to see the humor in a given situation. I also find it impossible to frown and laugh at the same time. I knew I had a problem with discipline long before the day I discovered my first-born, Zach, age three, engrossed in the contents of my make-up kit. With proper anguish and indignation, I confiscated his supplies and began the scrubdown.

Suddenly, he pointed his chubby finger at me and said in a

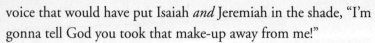

voice that would have put Isaiah *and* Jeremiah in the shade, "I'm gonna tell God you took that make-up away from me!"

"Well," I responded firmly, "God sees everything and He knows you took my make-up without asking me."

Silence. Then very quietly he admitted, "Oh. I not be frazy bout that."

Ah, discipline. Ain't many of us frazy about it. And kids know all the angles. The important thing, say the experts, is not to let them worm their way out of it.

At age two, reasonableness was not Zach's strong suit. If I failed to cut his peanut butter sandwich into a perfect right triangle, he would throw himself to the floor thrashing, screaming and nearly foaming at the mouth. To handle the situation without getting physical, I was faced with the prospect of hiring a professional draftsman to bring his protractor and Xacto Knife™ and cut the sandwich. The other possibility was to call the folks at the zoo to come with their tranquilizer guns.

My husband and I, without kerchief or cap, began to dream of a long winter's nap.

Neither alternative seemed really practical, so I faced the showdown, shades of *High Noon*. However, he must have seen the spanking coming because he stopped the tantrum virtually in mid-air. He wrapped his chubby little arms around my knees and lisped, "I wuv you. I give you big kiss."

What's a mother to do? Spit in his eye?

The books tell us the goal of disciplining children is to teach them to become self-disciplining. A few weeks after I had determinedly dealt with Zach's sandwich syndrome, I made the mistake of cutting his sandwich diagonally from top left corner to

bottom right rather than vice versa. I was pleased and surprised when instead of throwing his usual tantrum, he said with great restraint, "This is *not* funny, Mother."

Being new to motherhood and partial to any "natural" philosophy of raising children, I bought into the whole Earth Mother ideal. It goes without saying that I was one of those women who breast fed their babies until they were old enough to cut their own meat.

But when I got the literature on "The Family Bed," I felt relieved and reassured, since Zach spent most of his nights in our bed. Little did I dream how crowded our nuptial bed was destined to become. When Zeke made his appearance, I decided one night to try to persuade at least Zachary to sleep in his own big bed, offering an inspired suggestion.

"Zachary, wouldn't you like to snuggle up with this nice big Pooh Bear™?"

He took one look at the teddy bear bait and tearfully sniffled, "I'd rather snuggle up with a nice big mommy."

So, for several years following, the children would file one at a time into our bedroom at night like silent sleepwalkers muttering, "I had a bad dweam," or, "I cold in my woom," knowing I was a patsy for frightened or freezing children.

Scott and I were frequently waking up with a vague feeling of never actually having slept, as we clung tenaciously to the sides of our bed in areas the size of small tea towels. The children, however, remained sprawled in our bed while visions of sugarplums danced in their heads, so blissful were they. My husband and I, without kerchief or cap, began to dream of a long winter's nap.

Fortunately, I came to realize that a tender-hearted sucker does not always a good mother make, nor any sleep receive, and I

began to move from the Back to Nature to the Dare to Discipline genre.

Sooner or later, however, comes a day when our children echo back to us the words of discipline we have taught them. One evening some years back before our son Gabe joined us, and after a late bedtime fiasco on an evening with no relief from a late working, stressed for success daddy, I had come to the end of my patience. I ordered the boys to bed, plunked Rachel on the couch and sentenced her to lie there until I could get a grip on myself. I began furiously loading the dishes into the dishwasher, grumbling to myself all the while until, like a balloon out of air, I exhausted my anger. Rachel, noticing a quieting in the kitchen, bravely peeked over the back of the couch. She smiled knowingly and spoke in a most maternal tone of voice.

"Are you ready to behave now?"

The M.O.M. Awards
Nancy Kennedy

It's Mother's Day. You down cold coffee and soggy toast, ooh and aah over plaster hand prints, and stifle a smile at the home-made card that reads: "Roses are red, vilits are blue, moms are nice, and I am too. Happy Mudder's day moM."

Next you clean up the coffee spills and help your kids find clean socks. You empty the litter box and start a load of wash.

Now you're in church. You maneuver your kids into their seats, separating the kicker from the kickee and the bulletin grabbers from one another. It's time to recognize mothers of distinction. The pastor asks the oldest mother to stand. She gets a round of applause and a carnation. Next, the newest mother is asked to stand. She would if she could, but she's in the crying room...crying with her newborn. (Her carnation gets stuffed

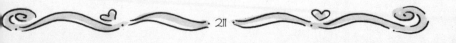

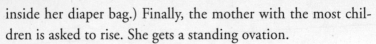

inside her diaper bag.) Finally, the mother with the most children is asked to rise. She gets a standing ovation.

Then there's everyone else, including you. You're not the oldest, newest or mostest. You've done nothing to earn recognition, and you wonder if anyone even knows you exist. For that reason the prestigious Mothers of Merit (M.O.M.) Awards were created for all the ordinary moms like you and me.

At this year's M.O.M. Awards ceremony, in the "How Does She Do It?" category, the first Mommy goes to you moms who simultaneously nurse your babies, stir cake batter, talk on the phone, wipe up grape juice with your feet and monitor homework.

Next is the "Only a Mother Would" category. This Mommy is for all of you who suck the salt off French fries before feeding them to your toddlers and consider a good day one in which you get to brush your hair *and* your teeth. You who regularly give the meatier pieces of the chicken to your husbands and kids—this Mommy's for you.

The Mommy for the dubious "I'm Turning Into My Mother" category is awarded to all of you who have ever said or done anything just like your mothers. This includes: 1. Saying, "I have a bone to pick with you"; 2. Tsk-tsking and finger wagging (preferably at the same time); or 3. Giving "the look."

The final Mommy in the "Is This All There Is to Life?" category goes to all of you who feel overwhelmed by the mundane tasks that make up your lives, who continually spill out your lives for your young ones, who willingly put your dreams on the shelf to serve your God by tying shoelaces and wiping backsides and

runny noses. Along with this Mommy, you will receive strength
for your tasks, purpose for your lives, grace to continue and the
satisfaction of knowing your service in the Lord is never in vain.
Happy Mudder's Day.

You Know It's Mother's Day When...

Martha Bolton

Mother's Day is that special day when we show our mothers how much they're loved. You'll know it's here when:

- A delivery man appears at your door with a dozen red roses, and he's not lost.

- Your children tell you how wonderful you are, and they're not setting you up for an allowance increase.

- You get served breakfast in bed. (Up till now the only way for you to get breakfast in bed was to sleep with a Twinkie under your pillow.)

- You notice your kids are hiding a card behind their backs, and it's not report card day.

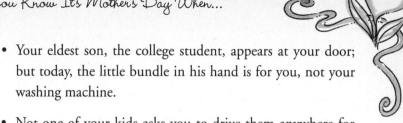

- Your eldest son, the college student, appears at your door; but today, the little bundle in his hand is for you, not your washing machine.

- Not one of your kids asks you to drive them anywhere for anything. (But since this is the first time in a year you've been able to turn off your car's engine, you find the key has rusted in place!)

- You get thanked for all the little things moms do throughout the year—you know, like cooking, cleaning, helping with homework, saving the universe…

- For the first time in months, you get taken to a restaurant where the "catch of the day" refers to their fish specialty, not how well you caught your order as you drove by their drive-up window.

- Your husband promises not to watch any sports events on television all day…as long as the game comes in clearly on his two stereos, ham radio, and Walkman.

- But most of all, you know it's Mother's Day when your family tells you what a loving, kind, warm-hearted person you are, and no one brought home a new pet!

you're never
too old
to laugh

Ancient Treasure
—FROM *OVER THE HILL AND ON A ROLL*
BY BOB PHILLIPS

An archaeologist is the best husband any woman can have: The older she gets, the more interested he is in her.

Forget It
Patsy Clairmont

I am the type of person who can walk from one room to another and not know why I've gone there. I know I had a reason when I began my trek, but I lost it on the way. Sometimes I try backing up in hopes it might come to me.

My family can usually tell this is the problem by the bewildered look on my face. Walking in reverse also seems to be a giveaway. Sometimes they try to help and other times they just let me wander aimlessly, figuring I'll wise up or wear out.

I try to blame this forgetfulness on age. But those who have known me for years remind me that my wires have never all been touching, although turning forty has seemed to loosen a few more.

I read in an article that after we turn forty, one thousand brain cells die each day. But according to the writer, it doesn't matter

because we have millions...or was that billions, anyway lots of them. My problem is the cells I've been losing were filled with valuable information I meant to retain—like where I'm going, how old I am, the names of family members, etc.

Names. Isn't it embarrassing when you know you know but you draw a blank? I realize that our names are important to us, and we don't want to be forgotten. That's why I think name tags should be mandatory. They should be pinned on us at birth and removed after the funeral. Think of all the awkward moments that could alleviate.

The guy, oh, what's his name, who sang "I Left My Heart in San Francisco" doesn't know how lucky he is. I left my bifocals in Indiana, my alarm clock in Ohio, my Bible on an airplane heading for Texas, my slip in Colorado, and heaven only knows where my watch is...probably with my sunglasses and keys.

Have you ever been digging through a drawer when all of a sudden you realize you don't know what you're looking for? If anyone is watching me, I just keep digging. I've found a lot of lost items that way.

It's disconcerting for me to dial the phone, and by the time the call connects, to find my mind has disconnected—I've forgotten whom I'm calling. Sometimes I hang up until I remember. Other times I listen in hopes I'll recognize the voice. Occasionally I've been brave and confessed to the anonymous party that I can't remember whom I dialed and hope they'll claim me.

The point I'm trying to make is...is...

What's Age Got to Do with It?

Pamela Shires Sneddon

Do an under-dog, Mommy!" my daughter Katie called out as she settled herself into the swing. She wanted me to lift her high, running beneath the swing as I pushed.

"I don't do under-dogs," I reminded her.

"Oh, yeah," said Katie with four-year-old matter-of-factness, "that's because you're an old mom. Only new moms do under-dogs!"

An old mom!

Katie's casual comment tore through my self-esteem like a toddler through a department store dress rack. I, an old mom? I was forty-one when Katie's twin brothers were born and forty-four when Katie arrived, but I'd never had the fact I was older than most of her friends' mothers laid out so bluntly. The shock was especially unnerving since in my own mind I actually had

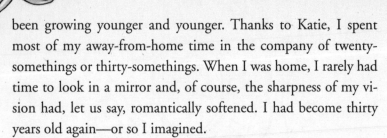

been growing younger and younger. Thanks to Katie, I spent most of my away-from-home time in the company of twenty-somethings or thirty-somethings. When I was home, I rarely had time to look in a mirror and, of course, the sharpness of my vision had, let us say, romantically softened. I had become thirty years old again—or so I imagined.

Katie's three little words crumpled the image. The lines around my eyes reappeared, my hair became grayer and I was, well, an old mom.

Since that day, I've become an even older mom. Katie is now a teenager. Along the way, I've learned some things are unique to the experience.

For those coming to parenthood from a fast-paced career, it may be a revelation to find it isn't always necessary to produce tangible results but to savor experiences. This change in perspective is among the many benefits of older motherhood, but it isn't usually rewarded in our culture. Sacrifices of time and energy for no immediately apparent outcome seem to go unnoticed and unappreciated. It's sometimes hard to remember there is value in putting a puzzle together ten times, wandering through the zoo with a two-year-old's agenda (or lack of), dipping every French fry and every bite of hamburger in catsup at a forty-five minute McDonald's lunch.

It helps to keep in mind, as one midlife mother put it: "... Five years from now your kids won't remember the night you left the dishes in the sink. But, they'll treasure forever the memory of the walk you took with them to look at the night sky." And so will you.

A midlife mom has challenges a younger mom doesn't. But she also has some pluses—besides the possibility of blowing out

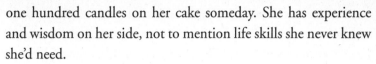

one hundred candles on her cake someday. She has experience and wisdom on her side, not to mention life skills she never knew she'd need.

At the performances of my daughter Katie's sixth-grade play, Bye Bye Birdie, I was the single exception to a no-parents-allowed backstage rule. The reason? I was the only mom who had first-hand experience with 50's and 60's hair-dos. One by one, I back-combed and, wielding a curling iron, crafted flips, French twists, ponytails or Big Hair with an expertise that amazed me—forty-some years had passed, but it all came back. When my daughter's schoolmates complained that the netting on the slips under their costumes itched, I told them what it felt like on a hot summer day to discover sugar water is not the best stiffening agent for net petticoats. "Yuck!" one fresh-faced eleven-year-old exclaimed, "I'm glad I didn't live back then!"

An older parent isn't allowed much slack to gripe and moan about the ravages of years.

In spite of such remarks, an older parent isn't allowed much slack to gripe and moan about the ravages of years. Regardless of how I might feel, or what I might see in the mirror, I'm kept from focusing on age-related aches and pains by the demands of those who assume I have limitless energy. Teenagers are especially good at keeping parents' attention off themselves. No matter how hard a day or how tired a mom might be, a teenager can always find something for her to do—or to worry about. Scripture records that Sarah laughed when she learned that she, a woman long past childbearing years, would have a son. It doesn't tell us the real reason God gave her laughter. It was to equip her for the time when Isaac would turn to her and say, "Mom, about your car…"

Sometimes when I've struggled through a long night, held together by prayer and cocoa, I'm tempted to envy the empty nests of my same-age friends. Then I think of what I would have missed. I wouldn't have known that a baby's touch would be as sweet to a forty-year-old mom as to one in her twenties—maybe sweeter, because an older mom is more aware of the fleeting nature of time. And at my age, I'd never have gotten to share screams of laughter on Disneyland's Splash Mountain unless begged by a twelve-year-old daughter to ride with her. I'd also not have experienced the exuberance of a teenage son bursting into my kitchen, shouting, "I need a hug!" rejuvenating me at a time when I was ready to retire from motherhood. And, what other fifty-something mom gets to stand at the back of a pulsating, darkened auditorium and watch her son play the drums; hearing through Kleenex-stuffed ears God in the beat, holding us all, even the pierced and tattooed individual bobbing a few feet in front of me.

At those times, I'm able to take a step back, to remember Psalm 127 and truly grasp that "children are a gift of the Lord" whether they come to us when we're young or otherwise, whether they fit the mold we've designed or not. Then I thank God for those lives He has brought into mine, for the chance to share the timeless mother-joy of Sarah and Elizabeth. And sometimes, due to a sudden unexplained burst of vim and vigor (or maybe a Starbuck's triple grande mocha valencia) I even feel energetic enough to attempt an under-dog.

The Good, the Bad, the Geezer

Charlene Ann Baumbich

This past May, George and I attended the college graduation of our baby. Although Brian actually finished school in November, Winona State University has only one ceremony a year. And since Brian is gainfully employed (Yippee! Yippee!) in Winona, and has become a Minnesota resident, we would be visiting his new home. Amazing.

On the way, I pondered how fulfilled I am, as wife, mother, writer, and woman. So much behind me, with so many days to look forward to, God willing. And I'm not even fifty years old yet. George and I are young empty-nesters and it feels good. Satisfying.

I pulled down the visor mirror only to slam back up the reality of crows feet and jowls. It's easier to feel young when you're not looking in a mirror.

It was a beautiful Minnesota day and the graduation was nice. There were over one thousand in Brian's class, and they read each person's name. Each graduate had his or her chance to walk across the stage and be acknowledged. I thought about how our names are recorded in God's book and was moved by the uniqueness of each person in that room, whether receiving a diploma, or watching a loved one graduate. So much hard work. So many hopes. So many dreams.

So much debt!

George sat grinning from ear to ear like a happy old geezer.

Evening delivered an opportunity for us to see Brian in a new light. A few of his friends threw a lawn party for the graduates. They all had wonderful senses of humor, conversation was lively, and they accepted our presence at the party with a warm welcome, making us feel like very cool parents. Very cool parents who left long before the party was over to hit the sack because we were tired, and, after all, parents.

The next morning George and Brian were golfing and left me to do some serious shopping. That evening we took a consensus and decided we'd dine out, then go to the movies. Us cool-and-young people, our son, and several of his friends.

Since I was in charge of the money this trip, I purchased the tickets at the window.

"Three adults for *Maverick*," I said. About the time the ticket person was sliding the tickets toward me, I heard George say, "No! Two adults and one senior."

"Right." I laughed and wagged my head at the ticket person.

"No, I'm serious. I just noticed the sign says their senior rate begins at fifty-five."

Save-a-buck George was thrilled to get a discount; I was mortified and quickly sliding into a depression.

"Oh my gosh, I'm married to a senior." Me, the cool, young, fascinating wife of a *senior*. I tried to distract myself with popcorn and a large diet cola, but even that didn't work. I missed half the dialogue in the show while fretting over this new discovery. George sat grinning from ear to ear like a happy old geezer.

"For better or for worse, for richer or for poorer, in sickness and in health, till death do us part." Aha! The loophole surfaces. "For senior" is never once mentioned!

Then I thought of my widowed friend. How she would embrace the opportunity to again pay for that love of her life—even at a senior discount.

Dear Lord, may George and I pay senior admittance together as Geezer and Geezette for many years to come.

Contributors

Carolyn Arends is an award-winning songwriter, critically acclaimed recording artist, and the author of *Living the Questions*. She and her husband, Mark, are the parents of one son.

Marti Attoun, mother of three, is a newspaper columnist and freelance writer living in Joplin, Missouri.

Charlene Ann Baumbich is an author, speaker, and humorist who invites readers to drop by www.dontmissyourlife.com to visit. She lives in Glen Ellyn, Illinois, with her husband, George.

Martha Bolton is a former staff writer for Bob Hope, two-time Angel Award recipient, Emmy nominee, and the author of more than thirty books, including *Didn't My Skin Used to Fit?*

Renae Bottom is a freelance writer whose work has appeared in such publications as *Christian Parenting Today* and *Marriage Partnership*. She lives with her family in Nebraska.

Patsy Clairmont, a featured speaker at Women of Faith conferences, is the author of numerous best-selling books, including *God Uses Cracked Pots, Normal Is Just a Setting on Your Dryer*, and *Sportin' a 'Tude.*

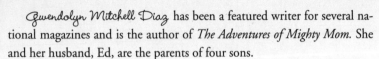

Gwendolyn Mitchell Diaz has been a featured writer for several national magazines and is the author of *The Adventures of Mighty Mom*. She and her husband, Ed, are the parents of four sons.

Bill and Pam Farrel are the codirectors of Masterful Living, an organization that works with couples. They are also the authors of numerous books, including *Men Are Like Waffles, Women Are Like Spaghetti*. The parents of three sons, they make their home in southern California.

Becky Freeman is an in-demand speaker and the best-selling author of numerous titles including the best-selling *Worms in My Tea* (coauthored with her mother Ruthie Arnold), *Peanut Butter Kisses and Mud Pie Hugs*, and *Chocolate Chili Pepper Love*. She and her husband, Scott, live in Greenville, Texas, with their four children.

Nancy Kennedy is the author of numerous books of humor and inspiration, including *Prayers God Always Answers* and *When He Doesn't Believe*. Her articles have appeared in numerous publications, such as *Christian Parenting Today*. She and her husband, Barry, the parents of two daughters, live in Inverness, Florida.

Karen Scalf Linamen is the author of numerous books, including *Just Hand Over the Chocolate and No One Will Get Hurt*. Two of her titles have been finalists for the ECPA Gold Medallion Award. Linamen, a contributing editor for *Today's Christian Woman* magazine and the author of more than one hundred magazine articles, speaks frequently at churches, women's retreats, and writers' conferences.

Mark Lowry is a comedian, musician, storyteller, author, and creator of the top-selling *Mouth in Motion* and *Remotely Controlled* videos. He appears in 150 events annually including touring with Bill Gaither and the Gaither Vocal Band.

Fran Caffey Sandin is the author of *See You Later, Jeffrey*, and a contributor to *The Strength of a Woman*. Her articles have been published widely in such publications as *Moody, Virtue, Focus on the Family Physician*, and *Home Life*. She and her husband, James, are the parents of three grown children.

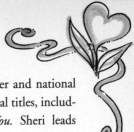

Sheri Rose Shepherd is a popular conference speaker and national spokesperson for Teen Challenge. She is the author of several titles, including *Fit for Excellence* and *7 Ways to Build a Better You*. Sheri leads Foundation for Excellence Ministries from her home in Oregon, where she lives with her husband and two children.

Pamela Shires Sneddon is a freelance writer, speaker, and author of *Body Image: A Reality Check*. She and her husband are the parents of nine children. They make their home in Santa Barbara, California.

Laura Jensen Walker is a popular public speaker and author whose works include *Dated Jekyll, Married Hyde* and *Love Handles for the Romantically Impaired*. She and her husband live in northern California.

Lynn Bowen Walker is a freelance writer whose work has appeared in numerous periodicals, including *Marriage Partnership, Christian Parenting Today, Moody, Glamour,* and *American Baby*. She and her husband, Mark, live in Los Gatos, California, and are the parents of two sons.

Tim Wildmon is vice president of the American Family Association, a Christian organization based in Tupelo, Mississippi. He and his wife, Alison, make their home in Saltillo, Mississippi, with their three children.

Source Notes

chapter 1: just kidding around

"What about the Grownups?" taken from *The Best of the Good Clean Jokes* by Bob Phillips. Copyright © 1989 by Harvest House Publishers, Eugene, Oregon 97402. Used by Permission.

"The Cheez Doodle Principle" by Nancy Kennedy. This article first appeared in *Christian Parenting Today* magazine (September/October 1997), a publication of Christianity Today, Inc. Used by permission.

"The Big Boo from the Balcony" excerpt taken from *The Adventures of Mighty Mom.* Copyright © 2000 by Gwendolyn Mitchell Diaz. Used by permission of RiverOak Publishing, Tulsa, OK. All rights reserved.

"George Invades Cyberspace" by Charlene Ann Baumbich. This article first appeared in *Marriage Partnership* magazine (Spring 1997), a publication of Christianity Today, Inc. Used by permission.

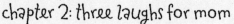

chapter 2: three laughs for mom

"Everyone Else's Mom" excerpt taken from *The Adventures of Mighty Mom*. Copyright © 2000 by Gwendolyn Mitchell Diaz. Used by permission of RiverOak Publishing, Tulsa, OK. All rights reserved.

"Mama Is a SCREAMER" is taken from *Out of Control,* Mark Lowry, copyright © 1996, Word Publishing, Nashville, Tennessee. All rights reserved.

"Minivacations Even a Travel Agent Could Love" taken from *Just Hand Over the Chocolate and No One Will Get Hurt* by Karen Scalf Linamen, Fleming H. Revell, a division of Baker Book House Company, copyright © 1999. Used by permission.

chapter 3: don't laugh at me because i'm beautiful

"Even These Hairs Are Numbered" excerpted from *Life Is Not a Dress Rehearsal* © 2000 by Sheri Rose Shepherd. Used by permission of Multnomah Publishers, Inc.

"Aromatherapy Overdose" by Renae Bottom. Used by permission.

"Held Hostage in the Dressing Room" taken from *Mama Said There'd Be Days Like This* by Charlene Ann Baumbich. Copyright © 1995 by Charlene Ann Baumbich. All rights reserved. Used by permission.

chapter 4: ten laughs, no weighting

"11 Tips to Survive Swimsuit Shopping" by Lynn Bowen Walker. Used by permission.

"I Never Met a Cookie I Didn't Fall in Love With" reprinted from *Prayers God Always Answers*. Copyright © 1999 by Nancy Kennedy. Used by permission of WaterBrook Press, Colorado Springs, CO. All rights reserved.

"Be a Loser" taken from *Sometimes I Wake Up Grumpy...and Sometimes I Let Him Sleep* by Karen Scalf Linamen, Fleming H. Revell, a division of Baker Book House Company, copyright © 2001. Used by permission.

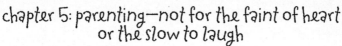

chapter 5: parenting—not for the faint of heart or the slow to laugh

"You Know Your Kids Are Growing Up When…" by Lynn Bowen Walker. This article first appeared in *Christian Parenting Today* magazine (March/April 1999), a publication of Christianity Today, Inc. Used by permission.

"All Mama Ever Wanted" is taken from *Out of Control,* Mark Lowry, copyright © 1996, Word Publishing, Nashville, Tennessee. All rights reserved.

"Missing the Manual" excerpt taken from *The Adventures of Mighty Mom.* Copyright © 2000 by Gwendolyn Mitchell Diaz. Used by permission of RiverOak Publishing, Tulsa, OK. All rights reserved.

chapter 6: blushing beauties —embarrassing moments

"Yuk It Up!" taken from *Normal Is Just a Setting on Your Dryer* by Patsy Clairmont, a Focus on the Family book published by Tyndale House. Copyright © 1993 by Patsy Clairmont. All rights reserved. International copyright secured. Used by permission.

"Blinded by the Light" excerpted from *Life Is Not a Dress Rehearsal* © 2000 by Sheri Rose Shepherd. Used by permission of Multnomah Publishers, Inc.

"Sure I Can!" taken from *Normal Is Just a Setting on Your Dryer* by Patsy Clairmont, a Focus on the Family book published by Tyndale House. Copyright © 1993 by Patsy Clairmont. All rights reserved. International copyright secured. Used by permission.

chapter 7: laughter, family style

"Pet Peeve" by Pamela Shires Sneddon. This article first appeared in *Christian Parenting Today* magazine (March/April 2001), a publication of Christianity Today, Inc. Used by permission.

"Honey, They Flushed the Cat" by Nancy Kennedy. This article first appeared in *Marriage Partnership* magazine (Winter 1998), a publication of Christianity Today, Inc. Used by permission.

"Would You Like a Coronary with Your Coffee?" taken from *Sometimes I Wake Up Grumpy...and Sometimes I Let Him Sleep* by Karen Scalf Linamen, Fleming H. Revell, a division of Baker Book House Company, copyright © 2001. Used by permission.

chapter 8: till death do us laugh —marriage humor

"Fun Questions for Married Couples" excerpt taken from: *Men Are Like Waffles, Women Are Like Spaghetti*. Copyright © 2001 by Bill and Pam Farrel. Published by Harvest House Publishers, Eugene, OR 97402. Used by permission.

"Would You *Let* Me Woo You?" used with permission from *Dated Jekyll, Married Hyde* by Laura Jensen Walker © 1997 Bethany House Publishers. All rights reserved.

"Time to Go: Ready or Not" taken from *Love Handles for the Romantically Impaired* by Laura Jensen Walker. Copyright © 1998. Used by permission, Bethany House Publishers.

chapter 9: a houseful of laughs

"Dare to Decorate" by Lynn Bowen Walker. This article first appeared in *Marriage Partnership* magazine (Spring 1999), a publication of Christianity Today, Inc. Used by permission.

"When You Can't Take It with You" taken from *If You Can't Stand the Smoke, Stay Out of My Kitchen* by Martha Bolton. Copyright © 1990. Published by Beacon Hill Press of Kansas City. All rights reserved. Used by permission.

"Handy Dandy Rooster Repairs" taken from *Eggstra Courage for the Chicken Hearted*. Copyright © 1999 by Becky Freeman, Susan Duke, Rebecca Barlow Jordan, Gracie Malone, and Fran Caffey Sandin. Used by permission of RiverOak Publishing, Tulsa, OK. All rights reserved.

chapter 10: bringing up laughter —more parenting humor

"Private: No Trespassing" taken from *Just Hand Over the Chocolate and No One Will Get Hurt* by Karen Scalf Linamen, Fleming H. Revell, a division of Baker Book House Company, copyright © 1999. Used by permission.

"The Outlaws of Physics" by Renae Bottom. This article first appeared in *Christian Parenting Today* magazine (March/April 1997), a publication of Christianity Today, Inc. Used by permission.

"A Hiding Place" taken from *If You Can't Stand the Smoke, Stay Out of My Kitchen* by Martha Bolton. Copyright © 1990. Published by Beacon Hill Press of Kansas City. All rights reserved. Used by permission.

chapter 11: humor with a shine

"Mapping Out Mom's Cleaning Strategy" by Marti Attoun. Used by permission.

"Chronic Purse-Stuffers Club" by Renae Bottom. A version of this article first appeared in *Marriage Partnership* magazine (Fall 1997), a publication of Christianity Today, Inc. Used by permission.

"It's Time to Clean Out the Fridge When…" taken from *Just Hand Over the Chocolate and No One Will Get Hurt* by Karen Scalf Linamen, Fleming H. Revell, a division of Baker Book House Company, copyright © 1999. Used by permission.

chapter 12: how quickly they grow, how swiftly we laugh

"Growing Up in Slow-Mo" taken from *If You Can't Stand the Smoke, Stay Out of My Kitchen* by Martha Bolton. Copyright © 1990. Published by Beacon Hill Press of Kansas City. All rights reserved. Used by permission.

"In the Throes of Mother Henhood" taken from *Eggstra Courage for the Chicken Hearted*. Copyright © 1999 by Becky Freeman, Susan Duke, Rebecca Barlow Jordan, Gracie Malone, and Fran Caffey Sandin. Used by permission of RiverOak Publishing, Tulsa, OK. All rights reserved.

"Future Mothers of the Groom Wear Radar and Keep Their Eyes Peeled" taken from *Mama Said There'd Be Days Like This* by Charlene Ann Baumbich. Copyright © 1995 by Charlene Ann Baumbich. All rights reserved. Used by permission.

chapter 13: you've got to be kidding —more family humor

"Angels Don't Always Have Wings" excerpt taken from *The Adventures of Mighty Mom*. Copyright © 2000 by Gwendolyn Mitchell Diaz. Used by permission of RiverOak Publishing, Tulsa, OK. All rights reserved.

"Stay Home—Alone" by Marti Attoun. This article first appeared in *Christian Parenting Today* magazine (September/October 1994), a publication of Christianity Today, Inc. Used by permission.

"When You Gotta Go" by Renae Bottom. This article first appeared in *Marriage Partnership* magazine (Summer 1998), a publication of Christianity Today, Inc. Used by permission.

chapter 14: mother, may i laugh?

"Learning to Land" excerpt taken from *The Adventures of Mighty Mom*. Copyright © 2000 by Gwendolyn Mitchell Diaz. Used by permission of RiverOak Publishing, Tulsa, OK. All rights reserved.

"The Fish Pond" taken from *Living the Questions*. Copyright © 2000 by Carolyn Arends. Published by Harvest House Publishers, Eugene, OR 97402. Used by permission.

"Acrylic Nail Tip Adventures" by Renae Bottom. Used by permission.

chapter 15: ignorance is (domestic) bliss

"Life's Grind (A Man's View of Ironing)" from *My Life As a Half-Baked Christian*, published by Promise Press, an imprint of Barbour Publishing, Inc., Uhrichsville, Ohio. Used by permission.

"Wish I Were Crafty" by Renae Bottom. Used by permission.

"Hen Hugs and Heart Tugs" taken from *Eggstra Courage for the Chicken Hearted*. Copyright © 1999 by Becky Freeman, Susan Duke,

Rebecca Barlow Jordan, Gracie Malone, and Fran Caffey Sandin. Used by permission of RiverOak Publishing, Tulsa, OK. All rights reserved.

chapter 16: to mom, with love and laughs

"Curbin' Their Wormin' Ways" is taken from *Worms in My Tea* by Becky Freeman with Ruthie Arnold. Copyright ©1994, Broadman & Holman Publishers. All rights reserved. Used by permission.

"The M.O.M. Awards" by Nancy Kennedy. This article first appeared in *CPT* magazine (May/June 1998), a publication of Christianity Today, Inc. Used by permission.

"You Know It's Mother's Day When…" taken from *If You Can't Stand the Smoke, Stay Out of My Kitchen* by Martha Bolton. Copyright © 1990. Published by Beacon Hill Press of Kansas City. All rights reserved. Used by permission.

chapter 17: you're never too old to laugh

"Ancient Treasure" taken from *Over the Hill and On a Roll* by Bob Phillips. Copyright © 1998 by Harvest House Publishers, Eugene, Oregon 97402.

"Forget It" taken from *God Uses Cracked Pots* by Patsy Clairmont, a Focus on the Family book published by Tyndale House. Copyright © 1991 by Patsy Clairmont. All rights reserved. International copyright secured. Used by permission.

"What's Age Got to Do with It?" by Pamela Shires Sneddon. A version of this article first appeared in *Today's Christian Woman* magazine, a publication of Christianity Today, Inc. Used by permission.

"The Good, the Bad, the Geezer" taken from *Mama Said There'd Be Days Like This* by Charlene Ann Baumbich. Copyright © 1995 by Charlene Ann Baumbich. All rights reserved. Used by permission.